SPECIAL NEEDS
in the primary years

Activities for including children with

Dyslexia
and language
difficulties

IDENTIFYING NEEDS • INCLUSIVE ACTIVITY IDEAS • ASSESSMENT ADVICE • PLANNING INTERVENTIONS

shops

the

went

I

to

DR HANNAH MORTIMER AND EILEEN JONES

Authors
Dr Hannah Mortimer
Eileen Jones

Editor
Victoria Lee

Assistant Editor
Kate Element

Series Designers
ʳah Rock/Anna Oliwa

Designer
Helen Taylor

Illustrations
Debbie Clark

Cover artwork
Katherine Lucas/The Organisation

Acknowledgements

The publishers gratefully acknowledge permission to reproduce the following copyright material:
Pie Corbett for the use of 'Wings' by Pie Corbett from "The Works" chosen by Paul Cookson (c) 2000, Pie Corbett (2000, Macmillan). **Eileen Jones** for the use of 'My Literacy Book' by Eileen Jones (c) 2005, Eileen Jones, previously unpublished. **Tony Mitton** for the use of 'Undersea Tea' by Tony Mitton from "The Works" chosen by Paul Cookson (c) 2000, Tony Mitton (2000, Macmillan). **John Rice** for the use of 'Leisure Centre, Pleasure Centre' from "Rockets and Quasars" by John Rice (c) 1984, John Rice (1984, Aten Press).
Every effort has been made to trace copyright holders and the publishers apologise for any inadvertent omissions.
Due to the nature of the web, the publisher cannot guarantee the content of links of any of the websites referred to. It is the responsibility of the reader to assess the suitability of websites.

Text © 2005, Dr Hannah Mortimer, Eileen Jones
© 2005, Scholastic Ltd

Published by Scholastic Ltd, Villiers House,
Clarendon Avenue, Leamington Spa, Warwickshire CV32 5PR

Visit our website at www.scholastic.co.uk

Printed by Bell & Bain Ltd, Glasgow

1 2 3 4 5 6 7 8 9 0   5 6 7 8 9 0 1 2 3 4

British Library Cataloguing-in-Publication Data A catalogue record for this book is available from the British Library.

ISBN 0-439-97189-6 ISBN 978-0439-97189-8

Activities for Including Children with Dyslexia and Language Difficulties

INTRODUCTION

Including children who have literacy (such as dyslexia) and language difficulties can be both challenging and rewarding. This book helps you to put inclusion into practice so that all the children benefit.

Aims of the series

There is a revised *Code of Practice* in England for the identification and assessment of special educational needs (SEN) that has been published by the DfES and this gives guidance on including children who have disabilities. In addition, the National Numeracy and National Literacy

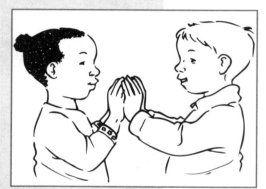

Strategies emphasise the key role that teachers play in making sure that the curriculum is accessible to all pupils. The Government's strategy for SEN includes a whole framework of initiatives to remove barriers to pupils' achievement and we are now beginning to see joined up policies that can make real differences to children. This series aims to provide suggestions to class teachers and others working in schools on how to meet and monitor SEN under the new guidelines. It provides accessible information and advice for class teachers and subject teachers at Key Stage 1 and Key Stage 2. It also provides practical examples of how teachers can use this information to plan inclusive teaching across the strands of the National Curriculum.

There is related legislation and guidance in Wales, Scotland and Northern Ireland though the detail and terminology is rather different. For example, the Statement of SEN in England and Wales is called a Record in Scotland. Nevertheless, the general approaches and information covered in the books will be relevant throughout the UK.

Within this *Special Needs in the Primary Years* series, there are five books on helping children with most kinds of SEN:
● Special Needs Handbook, which supplies general information for SENCOs or class teachers to help meet all the SEN in the school or class
● The Essential A–Z Guide to Special Needs, which provides basic information for class teachers and support assistants
● Activities for Including Children with Behavioural Difficulties
● Activities for Including Children with Autistic Spectrum Disorders
● Activities for Including Children with Dyslexia and Language Difficulties. These final three titles contain practical activities for including children with these kinds of SEN in the primary curriculum.

Including children with literacy and language difficulties

Most schools and classes will at some point include children who have literacy difficulties (such as dyslexia) or language difficulties (such as a specific language disorder). This book aims to provide a broad understanding of different areas of literacy or language difficulty and

show how primary teachers can make individual education plans for these children. The activity section provides practical examples of activities that have an inclusive approach to meeting those needs across the strands of the National Curriculum most affected by these difficulties.

Who this book is for

First and foremost, this book is for SENCOs, class teachers and support assistants who work on a daily basis with the children. The book will also be helpful for support professionals, headteachers and governors to use with the staff they work with. The SENCO's role is to support their colleagues in meeting SEN in their schools, though it is the responsibility of *each staff member* to support children who have SEN within their classes. This book will help SENCOs provide colleagues with the general information about identifying, assessing, planning for and including children in their classes who have literacy or language difficulties. Finally, the book will also be a useful reference for parents, carers and trainees.

Children with dyslexia

Many children who present with a dyslexic difficulty have also experienced earlier difficulties in language. Dyslexia is present when fluent and accurate reading and/or spelling does not develop, or does so very incompletely or with great difficulty. This is despite all the usual teaching methods, so you would not usually speak in terms of 'dyslexia' unless various interventions had been tried first. It is often referred to as a 'specific learning difficulty' since the level of attainments in literacy skills are much lower than one might predict from the child's intellectual ability or general oral ability. Dyslexia can take many forms and each child's learning profile will be individual.

Children with language difficulties

Some children in your school may have been diagnosed with a specific language disorder by a speech and language therapist because their speech, language and communication skills are developing in an unusual or very immature way. It is called a 'specific' difficulty because, although the children's language is disordered or delayed, their general intelligence and ability might be average or even high for their age. For these children, their understanding of language is usually affected as well as their use of language. Other children might be described as having 'expressive' difficulties in language relating to poor enunciation or a difficulty in co-ordinating the sounds within words. Often these children have quite subtle difficulties in interacting with the curriculum, and teachers need to be sensitive to their needs and make sure that they are included despite the barriers that their language difficulties create for them.

The scope of this book

This book has been designed to support teachers as they plan activities for children with both these sets of needs. There is an overlap in many of the *general* approaches for children with literacy and language difficulties. Teachers might find themselves having to plan additional and different approaches for children with *language difficulties* at Key Stage 1 because of their specialist needs. However, they should be able to include children at risk of *dyslexia* and other specific learning difficulties simply through their day-to-day differentiation. Good practice at this stage means appealing to all learning styles and delivering the curriculum in a structured and multi-sensory way, which is exactly what children at risk of dyslexia or other specific learning difficulty need. By Key Stage 2, some children with dyslexia may stand out as needing additional and different approaches. Some may even need small-group or individual specialist support and you will find yourself working with a support teacher or learning support adviser. At the same time, those children whose language difficulties have not

resolved will still need subtle attention paid to their language processing and understanding, and will benefit from many of the approaches you design for children with dyslexia. The scope of this book is to make suggestions *for including* these children in your daily activities and lesson planning. It is not to suggest specialist-teaching programmes for therapy or small-group support. There are more specialist publications for this listed on pages 95 and 96.

How to use this book

In Chapter 1, Inclusion, you will be introduced to the concept of 'inclusion' as it relates to children with literacy or language difficulties. In particular, you will see what the implications of these difficulties are for the child and for the teacher at different ages and stages. You will also think about some of the issues and challenges that face you when working with these children. There are suggestions for assessing children with different kinds of literacy or language difficulty in Chapter 2, Assessment. Sometimes different types of difficulty might call for different types of assessment and you will be helped to select the most appropriate method for your situation. You will also find a description of the legal requirements that you have to identify and support children who have SEN. Chapter 3, Planning Interventions, helps you to plan interventions for these children, working with their strengths and weaknesses. You will meet a wide range of approaches that colleagues in other schools have found helpful and you will later be helped to match these approaches effectively to your teaching activities.

Six activity chapters follow and these cover the six strands of the National Curriculum which are perhaps affected most by this area of need. If a child has a significant difficulty in literacy or language, then most will experience learning difficulties in the areas of English 1: Speaking and listening, English 2: Reading, and English 3: Writing. For

those with a specific learning difficulty, there may also be difficulties in Mathematics 2: Number and algebra, especially when it comes to recording number work, though others might be strong in all aspects of mathematics. Many subjects right across the curriculum will be challenging for those for whom literacy or language does not flow easily, and we have chosen the strands of History and Geography to provide examples of the kind of approaches you can plan. It is hoped that examples in these six areas of the curriculum will provide you with the starting points and ideas necessary for helping you deliver the entire curriculum in a supportive and inclusive way. There are two teaching activities for each age range of five to seven years, seven to nine years and nine to eleven years, each on a separate page. You will also find an introduction to each strand, covering how children with literacy or language difficulties are likely to be affected in that particular area of the curriculum.

For each teaching activity, you will find a 'Learning Objective for all the children' and also an 'Individual learning target' for children with literacy or language difficulties. There are also suggestions for 'Extension' (what to try if the targets were met) and for providing 'Special support' for the child with SEN. Throughout these activity chapters, you will find that words in italic can be cross-referenced to the interventions in Chapter 3, Planning Interventions, to serve as 'shorthand' for the explanations you met earlier in the book.

The activities have been selected to make a particular point for teaching children with literacy or language difficulties, reflecting the strengths, weaknesses, opportunities and challenges of those pupils. They should be adapted to suit the situation of each teacher and class and should act as a stimulus to trigger ideas for the teacher to adapt. Throughout the book there are photocopiable pages linked to assessment, monitoring and planning the activities and, at the end of the book, there are lists of helpful resources. You will find more detail about meeting SEN in the book *Special Needs Handbook* by Hannah Mortimer (Scholastic), also from this series.

Setting the scene

The activities described in this book encourage you to make use of a wide range of resources, materials and learning environments available in your school. The approaches have also been selected to make the child feel positive about new learning experiences and therefore grow in confidence. If you skim through the entire book first, focusing especially on the curriculum introductions and on the ideas for support, you will pick up ideas that you can transfer to different situations and different curriculum areas. After that, you may find it best to dip into the book as necessary, using it as flexibly as you need to.

Overview grid for ages 5–7

ACTIVITY TITLE	SUBJECT	INDIVIDUAL TARGET	LEARNING OBJECTIVE	OUTCOME
WHOSE VOICE IS THAT?	Speaking and listening	To attend to a short story with props and to join in a follow-up activity with confidence.	To act out own and well-known stories, using different voices for characters.	Children take speaking parts of story characters, using puppets.
I HEAR WITH MY LITTLE EAR...	Speaking and listening	To identify an object by its initial sound.	To secure identification of initial, final and medial letter sounds.	'Jump in the hoop' and a hearing version of 'I spy' are used to teach phonemes.
WHO AM I?	Reading	To learn single letter sounds.	To practise and secure phonic knowledge. To secure reading of initial letter sounds.	The children make their own letter cards to play a guessing game.
STAY SENSIBLE!	Reading	To read and use simple action words – 'running', 'sitting', 'standing' and so on.	To learn spellings of verbs with '-ing' (present tense) endings.	'Yes' and 'No' cards are used to answer silly and sensible questions.
HELP TEDDY	Writing	To form letters correctly.	To form lower-case letters correctly. To secure the ability to hear initial phonemes in CVC words. To read on sight familiar words.	The children teach the class teddy how to spell correctly.
WRITE AWAY!	Writing	To construct a simple sentence from word cards and copy it into a book.	To write and re-read own sentences for sense, spelling and punctuation.	A class book is created with each child contributing one page.
NUMERAL DETECTIVES	Number and algebra	To identify the correct rotation of numerals up to 9.	To write numerals from 0 to 9 correctly, tracing from top to bottom.	The children learn how to write numerals correctly by becoming 'numeral detectives'.
HOW MANY...?	Number and algebra	To understand and respond to words, such as 'more than', 'same as', 'less than', 'greater', 'smaller' and so on.	To use and begin to read the vocabulary of comparing and ordering numbers.	Cubes are used to compare quantities and the children create a graph of their results.
IN MY PAST	History	To use the past tense correctly when talking about past experiences.	To think about the past, using common words and phrases relating to the passing of time.	The children practise using the past tense by describing a favourite toy from when they were younger.
TRAVEL BACK IN TIME	History	To join in a simple role-play and speak in the role of someone else.	To learn about the main events and results of the Great Fire of London.	Role-play and the creation of a diary bring to life an historical event.
WATCH OUT!	Geography	To use and understand words, such as 'behind', 'on top of', underneath'.	To express views about making the area safer. To recognise ways of changing the environment.	Identifying hazards in the school environment encourages the use of directional words.
INSPECTORS ON THE LOOSE!	Geography	To enjoy early writing for a purpose.	To describe the features of the local environment. To express views on the features.	The children investigate their local neighbourhood and report on their findings.

SPECIAL NEEDS **in the primary years:** Dyslexia and language difficulties

Overview grid for ages 7–9

ACTIVITY TITLE	SUBJECT	INDIVIDUAL TARGET	LEARNING OBJECTIVE	OUTCOME
BABBLE GABBLE	Speaking and listening	To suggest missing words in a spoken story.	To improve listening skills. To describe and sequence key incidents.	The children tell a story in pairs and fill in missing words.
CHANGING PLACES	Speaking and listening	To interpret non-verbal signals.	To present events and characters through dialogue.	Role-play is used to explore body language and improvised dialogue.
INSTRUCTIONS	Reading	To read and act upon simple written instructions.	To read and follow simple instructions.	Current spelling words are hidden in a short text for the children to find, following given clues.
MIND-READING	Reading	To recognise the link between a mind map and the facts in a written text.	To identify the main characteristics of key characters, using them to write character sketches.	The children look at and create mind maps for a fictional character.
LISTEN AND LOOK	Writing	To hear and record the sounds within words.	To use spelling strategies, and to investigate and use the spelling pattern '-le'.	A spelling game of 'Odd man out' is followed by practising words with similar spelling patterns.
SPOT THE MISTAKES!	Writing	To identify and correct their own spelling mistakes.	To identify misspelled words in own writing.	The children write a piece of dictation and consider their spelling mistakes.
ADD IT UP!	Number and algebra	To calculate a simple tens and units sum correctly.	To develop pencil and paper methods for additions that cannot, at this stage, be done mentally.	In this activity the children achieve successful simple addition.
SNAKES AND ADDERS	Number and algebra	To understand and respond to words, such as 'half', 'quarter', 'fifth', 'percentage', 'multiple' and 'factor'.	To identify two simple fractions with a total of 1.	The children play a game where they match two sides of a fraction to make a total of 1.
READ ALL ABOUT IT!	History	To create a simple mind map based on a historical topic.	To develop understanding of historical events.	A mind map on the topic of the Romans is created taking information from a text.
A VOICE FROM THE PAST	History	To visit websites for specific information and to produce a simple written summary.	To find about the past from a range of sources of information.	The children gather information from a chosen website and write an article in small groups.
LEFT OR RIGHT?	Geography	To learn simple brain-gym exercises.	To use and interpret maps.	Maps of the local neighbourhood are used to create school walks.
MONKEY'S TRAVELS	Geography	To be motivated to engage in reading and writing for a purpose.	To learn about weather conditions around the world.	The children write a series of postcards describing weather based on real reports from a newspaper.

Overview grid for ages 9–11

ACTIVITY TITLE	SUBJECT	INDIVIDUAL TARGET	LEARNING OBJECTIVE	OUTCOME
SOUND DETECTIVES	Speaking and listening	To identify and manipulate letter sounds within a spoken word.	To investigate words which have common letter strings.	The children translate words from an alien teacher's mixed-up lesson.
RHYTHM AND RHYME	Speaking and listening	To demonstrate the use of rhyme and rhythm when speaking.	To perform poems in a variety of ways. To listen to and evaluate performances of poems.	A rhythmic poem is performed before the children write one themselves.
READ THIS!	Reading	To design and print an information sheet that is personally easy to decipher.	To evaluate their work.	Computers are used to demonstrate how texts can be made more reader-friendly.
BOOKWORMS	Reading	To enjoy reading chosen books with a partner.	To look at connections and contrasts in the work of different writers.	The children compose reviews of their favourite stories.
EXTRA–ORDINARY WORDS	Writing	To prepare a short piece of written work on computer for display.	To write a poem, making careful choice of words and phrases.	The children explore metaphors and similes and write a poem on the computer.
WRITE THE RIGHT WORD	Writing	To select the correct spelling from a Spell-Check menu.	To identify misspelled words; to apply knowledge of spelling rules, and to use dictionaries and IT Spell Checks.	Acting as editors, the children correct a journalist's piece of copy.
KNOW YOUR PLACE	Number and algebra	To understand which of two digits is in the tens place and which is in the units place.	To read and know what each digit in a number represents, and partition numbers into thousands, hundreds, tens and ones.	A game which teaches the children to understand the value of three- and four-digit numbers.
EQUIVALENT FUN	Number and algebra	To match simple equivalences such as half and 0.5.	To recognise the equivalence between the decimal and fraction forms.	The children convert fractions into decimal form.
CLOSE THE GAP	History	To make meaningful and grammatical additions to a partial text.	To understand why Drake circumnavigated the world.	The children research a topic to discover and fill in missing words in a text.
BREAK THE CODE	History	To translate a paragraph of text from code.	To appreciate the dangers and discomforts of life at sea.	A secret text must be decoded to find out about life at sea in the past.
TACKLING TRAFFIC	Geography	To present information in different ways.	To draw up reasoned plans to present solutions, proposing environmental change in an area.	The children discuss environmental improvements to an area in their locality.
TALKING GUIDES	Geography	To record an audio guide to describe natural conditions.	To learn how the environment affects the nature of human activity.	The children make an audio guide for young people planning a camping trip.

INCLUDING CHILDREN WITH DYSLEXIA AND LANGUAGE DIFFICULTIES

Some children have difficulties in reading, writing, speaking or processing language, help to understand their needs with this chapter.

Children with dyslexia

When fluent and accurate reading and/or spelling does not develop for a child or does so very incompletely or with great difficulty, children are sometimes diagnosed by an outside professional as having *dyslexia*. There could be many reasons why a child is not making adequate progress in literacy skills, including lack of

opportunity, lack of motivation or poor teaching for that particular child's learning style. Therefore you would not usually speak in terms of 'dyslexia' unless appropriate teaching and differentiation had been tried first.

Dyslexia is often referred to as a *specific learning difficulty* since the level of attainments in literacy skills is much lower than one might predict from the child's intellectual ability or general oral ability. Indeed, some outside professionals prefer to use the term 'specific learning difficulty' since 'dyslexia' sounds rather medical and implies that all children with dyslexia are the same. In fact, the difficulty with literacy learning is similar whether pupils have a specific learning difficulty or a general learning difficulty, particularly for pupils at Key Stage 1 in which *all* children are acquiring and developing their literacy skills. However, children with severe dyslexic difficulties may continue to find the process of reading or writing slower or less fluent than others at Key Stage 2 and beyond, even after appropriate teaching and support. At the same time, they can be highly successful in other subjects such as mathematics or science. There are many approaches and strategies that are going to improve their difficulties and remove as many as possible of their barriers to learning, and some of these are described in Chapter 3, Planning Interventions.

How many children are affected?

Up to ten per cent of children in the UK may be affected in some degree by a specific learning difficulty with about four per cent being severely affected (figures from the British Dyslexia Association). The majority of children with dyslexia are boys. The condition appears to run in families, but this is not always the case.

The main problems are usually one or several of:

- weak phonological skills (for example, linking words to sounds)
- poor sequencing skills
- poor auditory discrimination and memory
- poor visual discrimination and memory
- poor short-term memory.

When processing information, we all have to bring together information within the brain, organise it and make sense of it, and then be able to remember it and use it at will in the future. All these channels of thinking can be affected for children with dyslexia, with different parts of the 'chain' working more slowly than others. For most children with dyslexia, it is the *working memory* that is weakest, either for what is seen, what is heard, or both. The working memory is that part of the memory that has to hold on to input from the eyes and ears long enough to make sense of it, organise it and commit it to the long-term memory. When you are reading or writing, you rely heavily on this working memory in order to do so fluently. If the process is 'leaky' when you are reading, you will either make mistakes (poor accuracy), fail to understand what you are reading (poor comprehension) or take a long time about it (slow rate).

Specific learning difficulties

Dyslexia is just one of many kinds of specific learning difficulty and you will find that different professionals and LEA support services still use different terminology to describe a similar range of needs. This does not mean that they do not 'believe' in dyslexia – it is simply that each child is an individual; dyslexia can take many forms; there is a huge overlap between conditions, and the more general term sounds more inclusive. In this book, the term 'dyslexia' is used in its widest sense to include those children who have any apparent 'block' to their learning of reading, spelling or writing, despite the usual and appropriate teaching. Although some children with dyslexia may be in the top group for mathematics, you may find some have weaknesses in numeracy as well because of their weak working memories. For some children, the difficulties will be so minor that your usual classroom differentiation will meet their needs adequately. For others, you will need to plan individual approaches through School Action or even arrange additional tuition through School Action Plus. The diagnosis of dyslexia should not automatically mean that a child needs one-to-one tuition – the decision should be taken on the level and type of the child's difficulties (see Chapter 2, Assessment).

Some children have a genuine and significant difficulty in processing numbers and calculations and these children are sometimes diagnosed as having *dyscalculia*. Others have a persistent difficulty in handwriting and recording, despite interventions and help, and the term *dysgraphia* is sometimes used. The term *dyspraxia* (or *developmental co-ordination disorder*) is sometimes used to describe children with difficulties in processing spaces and shapes, fine-motor co-ordination and personal organisation. Although this book does not address these areas of difficulties, you will find that

many of the approaches overlap. The activity ideas for using multi-sensory and structured approaches are likely to suit all children, whether or not they have specific learning difficulties. The most important way in which you can help is to see the child as an individual learner with a particular set of strengths and weaknesses. Rather than be guided by a particular label, use your expertise in teaching and your knowledge of the child to address their educational needs through an individually designed programme. You will find an example of this in Chapter 2, Assessment.

Teaching approaches for dyslexia

The most inclusive approaches for supporting pupils with dyslexia will be whole-school and involve planning a dyslexia-friendly approach for everyone. The main thrust of the teaching approaches should be:

● to provide clues through several channels at once (multi-sensory teaching)
● to structure the learning step by step so that gaps are filled
● to use differentiation to ensure success
● to make allowances for the condition by giving more time
● to adjust the materials used (such as using larger font sizes, spacing or colouring)
● to provide opportunities for practice in order to acquire greater fluency and restore confidence
● to provide high intellectual stimulation but reasonable expectations for written responses.

You will notice that some of these approaches can be carried out in one-to-one or small-group situations that provide the child with a structured multi-sensory literacy programme. Others might be shared with parents and carers, such as the need for regular practice and the restoring of confidence. However, most need to be applied in the day-to-day classroom. You cannot assume that because a child is receiving specialist tuition (perhaps out of school) that their needs are being met.

At Key Stage 1, it should be possible to build all of these approaches into your day-to-day classroom teaching. After all, most children at this stage learn best through multi-sensory approaches that appeal to all three learning styles: visual, auditory and kinaesthetic. However, because of the extent of their gaps in learning and the more complex demands of literacy, some children at Key Stage 2 may be withdrawn into small groups for literacy support, or even offered individual tuition (sometimes out of school). If a child is also receiving tuition, it will be vital for you to link

your own approaches with the tutor's so that the child is taught with consistency and you can build on each other's teaching. Chapter 2, Assessment, will help you build an individual education programme around a child who is also receiving additional support.

This books covers what you can do as class teacher to support the child with literacy or language difficulties *in the classroom*. It does not cover the specialist approaches that can be applied during individual tuition.

Identifying dyslexia

There are various checklists that are said to identify children with specific learning difficulties such as dyslexia. However, these should only be used with care since most of the 'symptoms' are present in all children learning literacy skills and can be overcome with teaching, practice and confidence. You should only consider a dyslexia diagnosis if a child's difficulties have persisted for some time despite your usual appropriate interventions. For these children, these are the signs you might look out for. They fall broadly into four areas: language, auditory skills, visual skills and general development.

Language
● Often there is a history of delayed speech and language development. You might have noticed a difficulty (greater than the other pupils) in pronouncing multi-syllabic words clearly, perhaps with some speech sounds becoming reversed or substituted (for example, 'ephelant').
● Sometimes these children cannot retrieve words efficiently from their memory when they want to.
● Sometimes they have a difficulty in ordering and sequencing language when they speak in sentences.

Auditory skills
● These children might become easily confused by letters that have similar sounds (such as 'f' and 'v').
● They might be able to sound out words when reading but not blend them together to form words.
● They might find it hard to hear sounds within words, such as rhymes or alliteration – this is known as poor *phonological awareness*.
● They might find it hard to break words into syllables when reading or writing.
● They might find it hard to recall days of the week, months of the year or times tables.

Visual skills
● You will probably notice more than the usual confusions in letter order when reading and writing.
● There may be poor left-right discrimination with frequent reversals (such as 'b' and 'd'). Reversals should normally fade out by the age of six, though it can be slightly later for left-handers.
● Letters that look similar might be confused (such as 'n' and 'u'; 'i' and 'j').

- You might notice mirror-writing. This is not unusual at age four to five, though persists for longer for some children with dyslexia.
- Memory for high frequency spellings might be very weak.
- Spelling can be bizarre.
- Reading of 'nonsense words' can be very difficult since there are no contextual cues to make use of.
- Some children report that written print moves as they try to read it. These children might have a visual difficulty rather than a dyslexic difficulty and might be helped through the use of coloured overlays or spectacle prescriptions. There are more details on pages 95 to 96.

General development

- There can be evidence of clumsiness, particularly in the early days of school.
- You might notice a very short attention span.
- These children probably lack confidence and may have low self-esteem (as if they feel that the business of learning to read and write is a foreign language to them).
- You might notice 'good days' and 'bad days'.
- You might find spellings learned are lost soon afterwards or not generalised into everyday writing.
- You might notice that these pupils tire easily since children with dyslexia have to work harder than others.
- There may be a family history of dyslexia or weak spelling or reading skills.

Children with speech and language difficulties

Most children appear to acquire language and speech in a remarkably uniform way and seem to be almost 'pre-programmed' to acquire speech sounds, grammar, meaning and to want to communicate socially. Their whole language seems geared towards helping them find out as much about their world as possible. As they find out more and develop clever language skills, they become

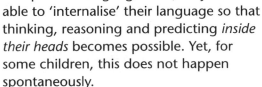

able to 'internalise' their language so that thinking, reasoning and predicting *inside their heads* becomes possible. Yet, for some children, this does not happen spontaneously.

Speech and language difficulties occur for many different reasons. There might be a lack of opportunity for development because of deprivation or emotional causes; there might be a hearing loss or physical disability, a general difficulty in learning and development, or difficulties even in the absence of these causes. This last group of children is sometimes described as having a *specific developmental disorder of speech and language, language impairment* or *specific language disorder.*

What you might observe

Whereas all children in the early stages of school are still mastering their use and understanding of language, you might feel that some have difficulties that go beyond what you might normally expect from their age and stage, even though they have had the opportunity to learn.

● Some children cannot speak clearly.
● Some have a very limited vocabulary.
● Some can only speak in very short phrases.
● Some can only understand very simple language and instructions.
● Some children cannot grasp the meaning of abstract language.
● Some cannot use language imaginatively or in conversations.
● Some do not understand what is expected of them in social situations yet.

Some children also have difficulties in communicating because English is not their first language; this book is not about these children, though some of the activity ideas may be helpful. Other children have language difficulties because they cannot hear clearly; again this book is not primarily about them although you will gather ideas for support.

Expressive language difficulties

Some children have learning difficulties because they *do not speak clearly*. Perhaps their language can only be understood by those who know them really well and where there is a shared context so that

the listener knows what the child is talking about. This might be because the child is slow to develop all the speech sounds necessary to make clear speech or perhaps they cannot co-ordinate the sounds in the required sequence. These children are sometimes described as having *dyspraxic*, *dysarthric* or *articulation* difficulties, depending on the cause.

Speech and language therapy can help them learn and practise new sounds and it is helpful if teachers can link closely with any ongoing therapy so that activities can be planned around the therapy goals. For example, some children benefit from activities that help them hear the rhythm of syllables and language. Number rhymes and action rhymes are most beneficial. The use of symbols, pictures or real objects can be used when the child is asked to make a choice or to plan their learning and play activities. Hearing back the correct enunciation of a word (without being asked to repeat it) can provide the child with the correct model of the word and also help the listener clarify what the child was trying to say. Patient listening and interpretation is called for, with plenty of opportunities for the child

to succeed in areas of learning that do not involve language. If their speech is *very* unclear, the speech and language therapist might recommend that they be taught to use a simple language programme with signing such as 'Makaton' (see pages 95 to 96). This is not used to replace their speech but to help others understand the words they are trying to communicate so that they can respond appropriately.

For other children, language remains shortened like a telegram because they do not naturally acquire the grammar and 'order' that language usually follows. Sometimes this is because their *language development is delayed* but nevertheless progressing along normal lines. Perhaps these children are delayed in other areas of their development as well and the language delay is just one part of this immaturity. Activities which help the child progress step by small step will be the most helpful, making sure that the child has a chance to succeed and develop confidence at each stage.

For other children, there is a *specific language 'disorder' or 'difficulty'.* For these children, their understanding of language (and especially abstract language, such as 'mysterious', 'empty' and other concept words) is usually affected as well as their use of language. You might hear these children described as having difficulties in language 'expression' and/or 'comprehension' or 'reception'. A speech and language therapist is usually involved and would be able to advise you on approaches. Sometimes these children will have been offered intensive speech, language and communication programmes at a speech and language unit when they were younger (usually during the Foundation Stage and Key Stage 1) and then return to their local school for ongoing support once they have overcome some of their difficulties.

Children with expressive language difficulties might use very short phrases or have difficulties in remembering the names of things. They might use general descriptions such as 'thing' rather than the label. Their speech might sound immature even though they have developed age-appropriate skills in other areas. They tend to lose fluency when they are excited or stressed, and talk best in a relaxed situation. Some children stutter and this becomes worse if they feel pressured or if attention is drawn to it. Again, your patience and sensitivity is called for and you should never jump in to complete their sentences for them. These children need your encouragement to slow down and regulate their speech in a relaxed and unhurried atmosphere.

Receptive language difficulties

Children with comprehension or *receptive language difficulties* can be difficult to detect. You might think that they understand everything you say yet, on close examination, you find that they are responding to a host of other clues rather than to the words alone. Test this out by offering no clues: 'Fetch your lunch box!' might well gain a response at the end of the morning session when everyone is getting ready to go into lunch, but would it gain the same response if you said it in the middle of a lesson?

Quite often, children who have specific language difficulties also have difficulties in understanding social situations; in seeing the other point of view; in using their imaginations; and in handling conversations. Many of the activities in this present book also aim to improve children's pragmatic skills. There are more ideas on helping children with *pragmatic difficulties* in *Activities for Including Children with Autistic Spectrum Disorders* (Scholastic).

How many children are affected?

Because of the differences between professionals in how they define the population of children with specific speech and language difficulties, it is difficult to be precise about prevalence. About three to 15 per cent of children in the UK experience some form of difficulty in acquiring language, though 40 per cent resolve these problems by the middle of their first year in school. Some children overcome an initial delay, but others go on to experience literacy and language difficulties if their early problems do not resolve.

In one study, 60 per cent of children who had language difficulties during their pre-school years continued to exhibit language problems at the age of ten and even beyond. The prognosis was poorest for those who had general learning difficulties as well. Your on-going assessment of how each child in your class learns and progresses will help you tease out those children who have general delay as well as speech and language delay and target your support for those most at risk.

The activities in this book for children at Key Stage 1 focus mainly on children with speech and language difficulties since these children who are significantly affected often need additional and different approaches at this stage.

At Key Stage 2, the learning difficulties experienced by a child with language difficulties become more subtle. Many will have overcome their most marked difficulties through speech and language therapy. It should now be possible for you to tune into what they are saying and to support them as they develop their literacy skills, following the usual wave of approaches in the National Literacy and Numeracy Strategies. For many of these children, it might seem on the surface that they have overcome their difficulties altogether. However, from time to time, you might find yourself surprised that they have not grasped the central meaning of what you are saying, they might not have comprehended the text they were reading or they might be finding it hard to retrieve words from their memories. It will take your sensitive assessment and planning to isolate those areas of learning that the child is still challenged by and focus on these areas.

In broad terms, many of the approaches you adopt will be similar to the multi-sensory approaches that you would use for the child with a specific learning difficulty such as dyslexia. Indeed, children who have had an early speech and language difficulty are more at risk than others to experience dyslexic difficulties later on. Therefore the activities in this book for teaching children at Key Stage 2 focus mainly around pupils with specific learning difficulties.

The importance of identification

Literacy and language pervade every aspect of learning in the school curriculum. Therefore it is essential to identify any learning difficulties as early as possible in order to minimise barriers to learning. Some literacy and language difficulties are quite subtle and difficult to detect – such as a difficulty in understanding abstract vocabulary or in distinguishing children who *cannot* write from those

who *will not*. Dyslexia often goes hand in hand with poor motivation and low self-esteem if the difficulties are not recognised and supported. Children with language difficulties can become easily frustrated and exhibit challenging behaviour if they are not helped to develop appropriate communication skills. Also, under the current Joint Council GCSE, AS and A level examination regulations, teachers are asked to provide evidence that a pupil's difficulties have been recognised and supported over a long period of time if they are to qualify for examination concessions such as an amanuensis or a reader. Your SEN records will become important sources of evidence for this. For all these reasons, early identification is most important.

Literacy and numeracy lessons

The DfES has produced guidelines on how to include all children in the Literacy Hour and Daily Mathematics Lesson and thus make the National Literacy and Numeracy Strategies more accessible (see pages 95 to 96). The guidelines have detailed information about how to plan provision in literacy and mathematics for children who have SEN, how to choose appropriate learning objectives, how to plan strategies for enabling children with different learning styles to access the curriculum and how to see all of this through into planning units of work in the Literacy Hour and Daily Mathematics Lesson. The 'graduated response' recommended in the SEN *Code of Practice* and covered in Chapter 2 can be mapped on to the NLS/NNS Three-wave Framework in this way:

Wave One: the effective inclusion of all the children in a quality Daily Mathematics Lesson and Literacy Hour

Wave Two: small group interventions for children who should be expected to 'catch up' with their peers, given this extra support

Wave Three: additional and different approaches under the SEN *Code of Practice.*

In Wave Three, you might feel that it is not in a child's best interests to work on the same activities and objectives as the class as a whole because their literacy or language difficulties appear to need additional or different approaches. These are the children who have SEN and for whom you might need to 'track back' to a more elementary programme of objectives, either at an earlier level of the National Curriculum or on to the QCA P scales, which describe children's achievements at each of eight pre-National Curriculum levels. The 'Including All Children in the Literacy Hour and Daily Mathematics Lesson' document gives you guidance for tracking back through the Frameworks and, as such, should be an essential read for all teachers. The SENCO should be able to support colleagues through this approach.

You will find the two-week planning sheets particularly helpful since they enable you to visualise 'real' children and 'real' needs in a classroom context, with practical suggestions for progression and also what to do if those suggestions do not work. For those of us who learn by visualising and doing, as well as by reading, these kinds of example are invaluable and will help you to see that you already have many special skills to call on when planning for children with literacy and language difficulties.

What the difficulties mean to children

Children who have a significant difficulty in either literacy or language are bound to experience learning difficulties in the areas of Speaking and listening, Reading, and Writing. Children with specific learning difficulties might also find Number and algebra challenging, particularly when it comes to coping with the organisation and lay-out of calculations, remembering simple number bonds or recording data. For these reasons, these curriculum strands have been selected for four of the activity chapters in this book. You will find two teaching activities for each age range of five to seven years, seven to nine years and nine to eleven years, each on a separate page. These activities should not be seen as prescriptive recipes, but they will give you a broad introduction to the children's needs and spark off your own ideas for including children with literacy and language difficulties in your daily teaching. Nor can the interventions be seen as the total solution to meeting these children's needs. You might decide that some of the children require more intensive and specialist support in small groups or one to one. In this case, you might find the reference list on pages 95 to 96 useful if you wish to improve your specialist knowledge of dyslexia and language difficulties.

Of course, subjects right across the curriculum will be challenging for those for whom literacy and language does not flow easily, and the strands of History and Geography have also been selected to provide examples of the kind of approaches you can plan.

ASSESSING CHILDREN WITH DYSLEXIA AND LANGUAGE DIFFICULTIES

Assess whether children need different approaches to support their literacy or language difficulties.

When does a child have SEN?

First, you need to remind yourself of the legal definition of SEN so that you can then apply this to your situation in order to decide whether or not the child with literacy or language difficulties should be included within your SEN approaches. After all, you will be meeting a wide range of needs already in this area as part of your day-to-day classroom differentiation.

Children have SEN if they have a *learning difficulty* that calls for approaches which are *additional to or different from* usual. There is fuller information on how and when to decide that a child has SEN in the SEN *Code of Practice* and in the *Special Needs Handbook* by Hannah Mortimer (Scholastic) in this series.

There may be some children in your class where there has been no diagnosis of dyslexia or language difficulty as such but where you feel that their literacy or language difficulties are causing barriers to their learning. When deciding whether or not a child has SEN, your informed judgement of whether these children are making adequate progress and whether you need to plan additional or different approaches is far more important than any outside diagnosis of

dyslexia or language difficulty. If you are going to include these children in your SEN approaches, their difficulties have to be *significantly greater than for other children their age*. In other words, you are expected to be able to include a wide range of literacy skills and language maturity within your class as part of your usual differentiation. Generally, you will already be catering for the needs of children who are learning within two years either side of the average span of attainments for your year group.

What are the legal implications?

There might be a few children in your class whose literacy or language difficulties have persisted over time and despite all your usual and appropriate teaching. These are the children who have SEN on account of their literacy or language difficulties. Where this is the case, then you should be guided by the SEN *Code of Practice*.

In practice, you are likely to be planning support through School Action if you are not working alongside outside professionals. When

you plan interventions working with outside professionals, such as speech and language therapists, learning support teachers, dyslexia specialists or educational psychologists, this is known as taking School Action Plus. For children with severe literacy or language difficulties, the support provided through School Action Plus may not be sufficient to ensure satisfactory progress. The SENCO, external professional and parents may then decide to ask the LEA to consider carrying out a statutory assessment of the child's SEN perhaps leading to a statement of SEN for the child. Only children with severe and long-standing difficulties go on to receive a statement of SEN, perhaps because they need more specialist provision than you can offer in school.

What do I do now?

You are likely to find yourself in one of three situations. Perhaps there is a child moving into your class who has already been identified as having SEN linked to literacy or language difficulties. Your way forward is clear. You should proceed to monitor the SEN and set a regular individual education plan (IEP), either as part of School Action, School Action Plus or as part of any statemented provision that has been set by the LEA. If the system is working as it should be, there should be information and programmes already available from the previous school or class. This should give you enough to plan your interventions, and you will need to carry out a fuller assessment before the next IEP review so that you can advise on whether additional and different approaches are still required.

Once in a certain phase of the SEN approaches (School Action, School Action Plus or even statemented), it does not mean that a child is destined to remain there. Movement between the different phases should depend on the needs of the child, present progress and current barriers to learning. There is more information about writing an IEP for a child with language or literacy difficulties on pages 26 to 27 and an example on page 30.

In the next scenario, you might have a pupil who has been diagnosed by an outside professional as having dyslexia or a speech and language difficulty. You need to make an informed decision based on the information available and you will need the support of your SENCO to do this. If there is a specialist report (perhaps from a dyslexia specialist), you need to look through this carefully. Are the scores and the recommendations in line with many of your other pupils who are not being monitored for SEN? If so, it is likely that you are already able to cater for this level of need through your existing classroom differentiation.

If you are given specialist information through a specialist report, you need to act on it and plan reasonable adjustments to your teaching.

If you are going to decide *not* to follow SEN approaches, you need very clear evidence as to *why* not, and you should make it absolutely clear that you are nevertheless able to meet the child's identified needs. If the scores and findings suggest that there are subtle underlying barriers to the child's learning, you would be wise to plan

SEN approaches through School Action or (if you are continuing to work with a specialist tutor or an educational psychologist) School Action Plus.

If a speech and language therapist has diagnosed a speech and language difficulty, you need more information on whether that difficulty might provide a barrier to the child's learning in class. For example, a simple enunciation difficulty might not affect learning and progress. A language disorder most certainly would, and you would be advised to monitor the child's SEN through School Action Plus, with the speech and language therapist having an input to the IEP and the interventions planned.

The third scenario is one in which you yourself have concerns about a child's literacy or language development and progress.

Perhaps you are identifying a child's SEN for the first time. In this case, you need to carry out a thorough assessment in order to identify what aspects of the child's learning require additional or different approaches. You will find some basic advice below and the school's SENCO will help you decide whether the results of your assessment suggest SEN approaches.

Assessing literacy difficulties

Here are some pointers for assessing a child's difficulties and supporting their weaknesses. Remember that a child only has SEN if the difficulties go beyond what you would expect for that pupil's age and stage and if they call for additional and different approaches to the majority of the children in your class.

Reading
● Does the child rely on pictures and contextual clues rather than gather meaning from the words?
● Is the child clearly uncomfortable and anxious when reading?
● Is the child able to recognise familiar words from a reading book when they are on a flashcard?
● Can the child tell the difference between different orientations and reversals of the same letter or group of letters? You will find a helpful assessment sheet on visual discrimination on photocopiable page 31.
● Does the child know each individual letter sound?
● Does the child know each common blend and digraph? You will find a checklist on photocopiable page 32. There is also a comprehensive list of letter groups for reading and spelling in the NLS and NNS publication *Including All Children in the Literacy Hour and Daily Mathematics Lesson*.
● Can the child sound out and blend phonically regular words that spell as they sound even if those words are nonsense (such as 'g-i-d' or 'pl-o-f')?

● Does the child simply memorise the text from hearing others read it first?

● When reading, does the child look at the first sound then guess the rest without scanning the word?

● Does the child lose place easily when reading?

● Are words added, omitted or substituted by another word that looks approximately the same (such as 'thought' and 'through')?

● Is attention paid to punctuation, expression and are the substitutions made still grammatically correct?

● Is the child able to understand what has been read and able to retell the story or answer questions on it?

You will see that a great deal of information can be obtained simply by noting the mistakes that a child makes when reading. This approach to assessment is known as *miscue analysis*. You can either tape-record the child reading aloud or listen to them read as you mark an identical text with their errors. This will help to plan an intervention built on that child's area of weakness – helping them become better able to use their visual judgements, their knowledge of word sounds, their memories, their use of context or their scanning.

Schools and teachers do vary in the approaches they use to teach reading. If a child is failing, then a *different* approach might be called for from the one being used at present.

Spelling

● Can the child write each letter sound and blend to dictation? Again, you can make use of the phonic checklist on page 32.

● Can the child hear each separate sound within a regular consonant-vowel-consonant word (for example, 'j-u-g')?

● Does the child reverse or confuse letters that look similar: b/d/p/q/g, h/y, t/f, m/w, n/u, s/z? (Reversals usually resolve by age six to seven.)

● Does the child substitute letters that sound similar: a/e/u, e/i, m/n, th/v/f, p/b, s/sh/ch, j/ch, g/k, n/ng?

● Does the child appear not to hear some of the sounds within the words (such as the 'n' in 'went', spelling it as 'wet')?

● Does the child telescope words, missing out some of the syllables (such as 'actly' for 'actually')?

● Are there almost bizarre mistakes as if the hand is not doing as the brain tells it (such as 'mistgc' for 'mistake')?

● Can the child copy spellings correctly underneath, from a card or from the board?

● Does the child resort to capital letters or printing when writing text?

● Does the child take a long time to write and spell?
● Does an otherwise motivated child become noticeably more distracted and disruptive when it is time to write?
You will see that you can do a useful assessment simply by looking through examples of the child's writing in a number of situations and then trying some dictation, targeting the letter groups and spellings that you wish to monitor.

Handwriting

● Does the child have poor pencil control even when not writing, such as when doing mazes and puzzles?
● Can the child form each letter correctly with appropriate joining strokes (such as the tail at the end of the 'a')? This needs early detection before bad habits are formed. You might find the assessment checklist on photocopiable page 33 useful.
● Does the child hold the pencil or pen correctly and apply the correct pressure?
● Does the child rush as if the brain is in a faster gear than the child's ability to write?
● Is the whole product messy, unsatisfying and difficult to decipher?
● Has the child developed a comfortable writing style yet with consistent size, slope and formation?
● Is the paper placed at a slight angle for ease of writing? This is especially important for left-handers whose hand will otherwise mask and smudge their work.
When assessing writing, you need to observe the child at work as well as collect examples of their writing. Writing involves a whole set of behaviours (hand position, paper position, pencil hold, pressure, level of attention, letter formation, cursive joins, persistence, organisation and speed of production).

Assessing language difficulties
Language processing

● Can the child recall a string of numbers spoken at one-second intervals? On average, most four- to five-year-olds can recall four digits, and most seven- to eight-year-olds can recall five.
● Can the child enjoy a story even without pictures to look at? This usually comes by age six.
● Can the child retell a familiar story or talk about an event? This usually comes by seven years.
● Does the child confuse certain words when speaking (record examples)? Common mistakes are words with similar meanings or associations, such as 'knife' and 'fork', 'cup' and 'tea', 'scissors' and 'cut'. Some children use their own jargon to replace certain words, such that only those who know the child can understand them.
● Can the child *label* abstract concepts (such as 'heavy') as well as *indicate* the concept ('Show me the heavy one.')? Again, examples are useful and will help you teach to the gaps.
● Are you absolutely sure that a child understands the words being read and talked about? Check regularly for meaning and keep a record of mistakes and weak vocabulary.

● Does the child have a difficulty in retrieving words from memory, tending to resort to generalisations instead (such as 'thingy') or to become frustrated? Note examples.

● Are verb tenses confused (such as, 'I did it tomorrow.')?

● Do words in the sentence tend to be spoken in the wrong order (such as, 'Mum helps out me!')?

● Does the child have difficulty processing a sequence of two or three instructions (such as, 'Stand up, fetch your book bag and go on to the mat.')?

● Can the child understand jokes, metaphors, idioms, euphemisms and proverbs (perhaps misunderstanding owing to a very literal interpretation of language)? Keep examples.

● Does the child pick up hidden meaning, nuances, facial expression, body language and tone of voice? Experiment in different situations.

Speech production

● Is there a history of early speech or hearing difficulties (talk with parents and carers and look at school records)?

● Has the child ever received speech and language therapy? What was the outcome?

● Is the child's current level of hearing normal? Ask the school nurse or health visitor to arrange a check if in doubt.

● Does the child mispronounce words? Which words (take examples)? Most children stop mispronouncing s/th and f/th by age seven. Words with several syllables may be especially problematical (such as 'hostipal' for 'hospital').

● Does the child confuse certain sounds when speaking (take examples)? Common mistakes are words like 'lemon'/'melon', 'aminal'/'animal', and Spoonerisms (such as 'flutterby' for 'butterfly'). Again, this would not be unusual before age seven.

● Can the child repeat back a word or phrase correctly (do this in a one-to-one setting in order to reduce self-consciousness)?

● Does the child only speak in certain situations? Collect a tape recording of the child's speech in the best situation if you can, in order to see whether speech and language otherwise appears to be normal.

● Does the child stammer or stutter? When is this worst? When is it not a problem?

Target setting

All children with literacy or language difficulties whose needs are being monitored under your SEN procedures need an individual education plan (IEP). This is a plan that should lead to the child making progress and it only includes those aspects of the teaching and learning that are *additional and different*. First, you should *formulate* a plan. You can then *implement* your plan over a period of time and *monitor* how effective it is in meeting the child's needs. This evidence allows you to *evaluate* the effectiveness of your interventions. Your task is not to 'cure' the child's condition of dyslexia or specific language disorder – it is to remove as many

barriers to progress as you can and provide stategies for progression despite the child's condition.

An example of an IEP is shown on page 30. There is also a photocopiable form which you can adapt for your situation on page 34. This plan should be reviewed regularly with the parents or carers and seen as an integrated aspect of the curriculum planning for the whole class.

Each IEP should contain three or four clear learning targets which the child can be expected to achieve with support. It should be reviewed regularly with parents and carers and you should always build in the support needed at home to ensure progress. These reviews will usually be arranged and chaired by the SENCO.

Children with SEN should become progressively more involved in setting and evaluating targets through their individual education plans. Talk them through their learning targets and agree together how you will know that the targets have been successfully achieved. Build in targets that the child themself is particularly keen to reach, breaking these down into easier steps if necessary to help them achieve it. Gather the child's own views on what has been most helpful and what has not.

Sometimes children are only too aware of their weaknesses but desperate not to appear different from their friends. Consider ways in which any additional support can be delivered discreetly and sensitively.

How can I get support?

Most local education authorities (LEAs) employ learning support teachers. These professionals are sometimes based at LEA offices but are increasingly being delegated to school clusters. They do not become involved just because a child has been labelled as 'dyslexic' but because you feel that the child has significant learning difficulties affecting literacy or numeracy. This is a far more pragmatic way of working since the approaches for children with literacy and numeracy difficulties are similar whether those difficulties are specific or general.

Many LEAs also have specialist language teachers who provide outreach support, sometimes based in specialist speech, language and communication units. You will find these professionals particularly useful since they are aware of the National Curriculum and how children with speech and language disorder are affected right across the board. Even if a speech and language therapist is no longer involved, they can advise you on the more subtle residual learning difficulties that a child with earlier language problems might still have.

You will find that many children with speech and language disorders are still being monitored by a speech and language therapist. These professionals are sometimes employed by the LEA though more often based within NHS clinics and services. Often their approach is one of working through parents and teachers rather than providing direct therapy, since all language must take place within a social context.

Help parents to understand that they are not being short-changed if direct therapy is not advised – the indirect approach really does work best providing you are given regular advice yourselves and you have the resources to see the recommendations through. Sometimes it is that very need for extra resources to maintain a recommended speech and language programme that leads the school to request statutory assessment in the hope of obtaining additional learning support assistance in class. Sometimes this kind of support is available on a cluster basis without the need for statutory assessment. Your SENCO will know which is the case for you.

The other source of support that might be available to you is a voluntary organisation or private dyslexia service. The Dyslexia Institute provides assessment and tuition on a private basis and parents may opt to use this kind of service if their child's needs are not significant enough to be assessed through the LEA. You can obtain much useful general information about dyslexia, suitable interventions and resources from the dyslexia organisations (see full details pages 95 to 96).

Private assessment works best when the specialist contacts the school beforehand to gather information about the child's school progress and where class teachers see the report and recommendations afterwards. Because this is usually a private arrangement between parents and specialist, you will probably find yourself having to make any links with the external professional through the parents themselves. If tuition is offered, then do your utmost to make sure it links into what you are doing in class so that the child's needs are being met at all levels.

Remember that whether or not a child has SEN depends on whether additional or different approaches are needed, not on whether there is a label.

Translating needs to others

Once you have decided that a child has SEN on account of literacy or language difficulties, it would be helpful if you could translate the child's needs for the other adults who live and work with them. This is a helpful way of 'getting your head around' what kind of general support the child will need day to day. Here is an example for a child with dyslexia. It was shared with parents and carers, learning support assistants and other subject teachers who worked with the child in primary school.

Gemma S. (age 10)   **Information for others**

Gemma has a specific learning difficulty – dyslexia. In her case, it means that she finds it hard to read or write as fluently as most of the others in her class. She also finds it hard to organise her ideas on to paper and has a poor memory for what she has just seen or heard. It is not her fault. It does not mean that she is slow in her thinking and reasoning – in fact, she is a very bright pupil with some excellent ideas to share. Her confidence is low and she tends to 'give up' rather quickly when she is writing because she feels she is failing. You can help by:

- writing down unfamiliar subject words for her
- not asking her to read out loud in front of others
- helping her think through her ideas before setting them down on to paper
- allowing her more time to copy from the board or finding an alternative method, such as letting her use a sheet to copy from or giving her a photocopy
- expecting rather less written work than from the others
- encouraging her to use her phonic spelling book
- breaking down literacy tasks into smaller steps for her
- marking written work for content rather than spelling
- tackling spellings separately using the SOS approach
- encouraging her to join in orally, and use strong praise
- allowing her to read back written work to you if it is unintelligible
- encouraging the use of tape recorders and ICT
- consider giving her written information sheets (well spaced and with colour highlights) rather than expecting her to take notes
- allowing her to word-process any project work.

Thank you for your help.

Mrs T
(Class teacher)

The National Numeracy and Literacy Strategies

You will find a wealth of detailed information in the DFES publication *Including All Children in the Literacy Hour and Daily Mathematics Lesson* and it is well worthwhile familiarising yourself with its contents. As well as helping you plan approaches under the Three Waves, there is detailed information about what you should be teaching all children and, therefore, when to come to the conclusion that additional or different approaches are called for. Even for children whose literacy and numeracy difficulties are so great that they cannot achieve the key objectives for Year 1 on the Standard Attainment Tests (SATs), you will be helped to track back using the 'P scales' so that you can include these children also.

For pupils who cannot write and record at the same level as the others, there is a pull-out poster to remind you of all the alternative methods you can use, including peer scribing, using alternative communication methods, using tape recorders, mind mapping, word storming, visual displays, sorting, making use of ready-made text and word cards, and using ICT. Many of these interventions are discussed in the next chapter.

EXAMPLE INDIVIDUAL EDUCATION PLAN

Name: Tomas   **Age:** 9   School Action Plus

Strengths: Tomas has excellent oral skills and has a lot of ideas to offer in class discussions. He is popular with his peers and a thoughtful member of the group.

Nature of difficulty: Tomas has great difficulties in organising his thoughts on to paper. He works slowly, fails to complete written tasks and becomes easily distracted. Tomas is not fluent when reading and struggles to make sense out of the text. Tomas has been diagnosed by the specialist learning support teacher as having dyslexic difficulties. These affect his reading, spelling, writing and some aspects of his mathematics (times tables and basic number bonds).

Professionals involved: Sue Johnson – Learning Support Service

Targets for this term:
- Tomas will correctly spell the three- and four-letter words from the Keywords list (75% success)
- Tomas will complete short passages of independent writing using appropriate sound-symbol correspondence so that the passages are decipherable to others (90% decipherable)
- Tomas will master and use the word endings '-are', '-ere', '-out', '-ain', '-ght' using mnemonics (eg: '-ght' – green-headed turtles) (75% success during tutorials, 50% success in class work)
- Tomas will begin to read fact and fiction material for pleasure.

How these will be worked on:
- continue with the worksheets from his present phonics programme
- keyword lists with SOS approach for learning spellings
- check knowledge of basic sounds and use magnetic letter board, variety of writing media, invent personalised mnemonics
- continue with his shared tuition for 20 minutes, three times a week
- full reassessment by learning support teacher prior to next review

Help from parents:
- word games to be sent home regularly
- continue with shared reading.

Review meeting with parents:
Last Tuesday of term 11.15am.

Who else to invite:
Learning support teacher.

Visual discrimination assessment

Ask the pupil to indicate which ones match the pictures, letters and words in the first column.

Reference						
🚗	🚗	🚗	🚗	🚗	🚗	🚗
↗	↙	↗	↖	↙	↘	↗
b	b	p	d	g	b	p
big	pig	dip	big	dig	gib	big
no	au	oi	io	ia	ou	ai
read	raid	reid	road	rade	read	rode
though	through	thought	throughout	though	thorough	tough

Phonic checklist

Use to check either reading (by writing them on to flashcards), identifying ('Show me the...') or writing in dictation (by building phonically regular words round them). You might find it helpful to make three photocopies and use each to record different skills.

single sounds:	f h k l j g d a q e t u s o p i y r w z c b m n v x
initial consonant blends:	st- br- dr- fr- gr- pr- tr- cr- bl- cl- fl- gl- pl- sl- sm- sn- sp- sk- sw- tw-
final consonant blends:	-st -nd -ng -lt -mp -sk -lk -ft -nk -nt
consonant digraphs:	ch sh th
triple initial blends:	scr- shr- spl- str-
vowel digraphs:	ee oo ea er ou ir ur ow ai ay ar aw or oi oy oa au ie ew
silent 'e':	o...e u...e i...e a...e e...e
silent letters:	w k b h u c
longer word endings:	-tion -sion -ture -ous -ious -ght
compound words:	rainbow seatbelt anywhere beetroot (and so on)
polysyllabic words:	wonderful telephone remember raspberry (and so on)

SPECIAL NEEDS **in the primary years: Dyslexia and language difficulties**

Handwriting checklist

Name of pupil:	Class/group:

Make four copies and record with a tick if the child can trace over the top of the letter/copy it beneath/write it to dictation/use it in free writing correctly.

single letters

'c' shapes: a ☐   c ☐   d ☐   g ☐   o ☐   q ☐

'n' shapes: h ☐   m ☐   n ☐   p ☐

'l' shapes: i ☐   l ☐   t ☐   u ☐   v ☐   w ☐   y ☐

others: b ☐   e ☐   f ☐   j ☐   k ☐   r ☐   s ☐

       x ☐   z ☐

bottom joins in cursive script

'c' shapes: a ☐   c ☐   d ☐   g ☐   o ☐   q ☐

'n' shapes: h ☐   m ☐   n ☐   p ☐

'l' shapes: i ☐   l ☐   t ☐   u ☐   v ☐   w ☐   y ☐

others: b ☐   e ☐   f ☐   j ☐   k ☐   r ☐   s ☐

       x ☐   z ☐

top joins in cursive script

'c' shapes: a ☐   c ☐   d ☐   g ☐   o ☐   q ☐

'n' shapes: h ☐   m ☐   n ☐   p ☐

'l' shapes: i ☐   l ☐   t ☐   u ☐   v ☐   w ☐   y ☐

others: b ☐   e ☐   f ☐   j ☐   k ☐   r ☐   s ☐

       x ☐   z ☐

INDIVIDUAL EDUCATION PLAN

Name:	Date of birth:	School Action/School Action Plus/Statement

Strengths:

Nature of difficulty:

Professionals involved:

Targets for this term:

How these will be worked on:

Help from parents:

Review meeting with parents:

Who else to invite:

PLANNING INTERVENTIONS

Use your own expertise to mix and match a range of interventions to support children with difficulties.

Interventions for including children with dyslexic difficulties

There are many practical interventions that you can mix and match for children with dyslexia, literacy or language difficulties in order to build on their strengths and make the most of the opportunities and challenges that arise. Each approach suggested is given a title that will reappear in the activity chapters of the book. In this way, you can cross-reference support ideas to actual approaches and have several ideas up your sleeve depending on the nature of the child's difficulty and your own context. No one intervention will suit every child and each child will need a range of interventions. You should make sure your approaches dovetail with work being carried out by a specialist tutor or speech and language therapist. This chapter has two sections: 'Interventions for including children with dyslexic difficulties' and 'Interventions for including children with language difficulties'.

Working with strengths
Alternative means of recording
You will find a helpful pull-out sheet at the back of the DFES publication *Including All Children in the Literacy Hour and Daily Mathematics Lesson*. For pupils who find it hard to record their ideas in writing, consider asking them to create displays or posters, make digital photo spreads, create mind maps or flow charts, or present their work on video or tape. Sometimes children can work with a partner, dictating and scribing. Sometimes multiple-choice answers can be highlighted or labels matched to texts and pictures.

Encourage oral responses
Make sure that pupils with dyslexia have plenty of opportunities to shine in front of their peers in practical and oral work. Suggest the use of a tape recorder or Dictaphone for recording ideas during project work.

Highlighting

Encourage the use of highlighting to mark salient points. Give the child a set of highlighters for marking their own notes. Help the child highlight prior to any learning or revision activity.

Pictograms

Some literacy programmes (such as 'Letterland' and 'Jolly Phonics', see pages 95 to 96) make use of letter/picture combinations to help children at Key Stage 1 remember their letter sounds. You may find the 'Picture alphabet' on photocopiable page 45 helpful. Enlarge the sheet to A3 size, cut up the letters and ask the children to colour them. Then, mount them on to card and laminate. Use them in a fishing game (see page 48) or as flashcards.

Mind maps

Let the children use different forms of presenting their work, such as by drawing a mind map or handing in bullet-point notes. Mind maps are webs of ideas and can be done in different colours with illustrations as well as words. On page 46 there is an example of a mind map on the subject of study skills. You can use it both as an example of mind mapping and as a revision aid for pupils.

SMC teaching: Structured, Multi-sensory and Cumulative

This is a simple step-by-step approach that is:
● structured – follows all the skills that have to be acquired in a logical and comprehensive way
● multi-sensory – uses every sense so that different connections are strengthened in the brain, weaknesses are compensated for and fluency and recall improved
● cumulative – allows each skill to build on the one before so that confidence and attainments build progressively.
You can make use of commercially available support programmes (see pages 95 to 96) or adapt your own based on the DFES publication *Including All Children in the Literacy Hour and Daily Mathematics Lesson.*

Use ICT

Encourage the child to word-process work so that it is pleasingly presented. It is extremely useful for children with dyslexia to learn keyboard skills from the earliest age so that they have another way of remembering spelling – the motor movements made by their fingers when typing. The use of editing tools and spell checks are also helpful. ICT software is useful for those who struggle with writing and can be used to develop reading and spelling skills.

Working with weaknesses
Allow time

Do not expect quite as much written work or homework and allow more time for copying off the board. Children with dyslexia may make considerable progress yet may always be slow to read, write or both. This is not their fault.

Be discreet

Do not insist the child reads out loud in front of the class. If you have to monitor a particular child's reading progress, make sure that other children cannot overhear. Marking homework or written work with a discreet, 'Well done – please see me' can be far more productive than writing pages of corrections and comments for a pupil who might struggle to read your writing or become discouraged by all the red ink.

Break steps down

Let the child sit where you can provide help unobtrusively. Break written tasks into smaller steps and help the child organise work before it is begun. A small amount of individual attention from you before work is started can save a great deal of recovery work later. Provide new spellings in advance of new topic work.

Clever colours

Some pupils with visual reading weaknesses (such as a scanning difficulty) find that certain coloured paper or certain types and size of font are much easier for them to read. Why not use this as a project and let the children do the research themselves? You can then adjust printed handouts accordingly. Other children may actually be given a tinted-spectacle prescription or coloured overlay by an orthoptist (see pages 95 to 96).

Phonological awareness

Make time to play and enjoy rhymes, to listen to the sounds within words, to clap syllables, and to improve phonological awareness. Most literacy schemes now build this in as part of the process of improving reading and writing skills. For some children with dyslexia, this is an area of particular weakness.

Sequencing skills

For others, sequencing skills may be especially weak. Talk through your daily routines and sequences, using picture cards if necessary, to show what happens next. Encourage the children to retell stories and experiences, gradually building up to longer sequences with a beginning, a middle and an end. Cut up simple picture stories or comic strips for the child to re-assemble in the correct sequence. Set up a mystery message using magnetic letters on a board but make deliberate errors in the sequence of some of the letters. Challenge the child to find and rearrange the mistakes.

SOS (Simultaneous Oral Spelling technique)

This is a multi-sensory method of learning spellings and can be easily shared with parents or carers for supporting the learning of spellings at home. First the adult writes the word and says it to the child. The child looks at it and repeats the word. The child then spells the word out loud saying all the letter sounds. The child then copies the word (in cursive script if possible), sounding the letters as they are written. The child reads the written word and then writes over the word,

saying the letter sounds. Finally, the child covers the written word and writes it from memory, continuing to say the letters in correct sequence. The child checks the written attempt with the original.

Small-group tuition

Talk to the SENCO if you feel that small-group or individual tuition is necessary. Most LEAs have now delegated learning support to local school clusters and you should find out what level of support is available in your area. Sometimes support teachers come in to advise class teachers on their approaches. At other times, the support teacher or SENCO will take a small group for specialist literacy teaching. In other schools still, pupils might be withdrawn to attend special units or tutorials at dyslexia centres. Creative use of classroom assistance (when available!) or parent help can sometimes release *you* to spend time with a small group of children.

Spelling aids

Provide spelling aids such as phonetic dictionaries – for example, the *ACE Dictionary* by Mosely and Nicol (LDA). Some pupils enjoy (and can manage not to become too distracted by) electronic spelling aids such as the 'Franklin Elementary Spellmaster' from Electronic Learning Products.

Working with opportunities

Build self-esteem

Do your best to avoid a feeling of failure so that the child does not become frustrated. Encourage the child to present their creativity in other ways. Talk through with the children how they see their difficulty and help them to understand that it is not their fault. Point out that in the USA, there are regular advertisements for 'dyslexic architects' because people with dyslexia often have strengths in creativity and design!

Cloze procedure

Provide a written text in which certain words have been omitted. Encourage the pupils to work with a partner to decide on the best word to fit in. This encourages the use of context as a reading strategy.

Individualise texts

Provide enlarged photocopies of any worksheets that carry a lot of dense text or reprint them with double spacing – this makes them easier to scan. If pupils have a lot of written copying to be done in a lesson, provide a photocopy of the text for the child with dyslexia to keep instead.

Musical sequences

Music seems to assist memorising. Look for musical times-table tapes and consider singing a daily alphabet song with Key Stage 1 children. Collect songs that recite days of the week or months of the year – or make your own up with the children.

Teach study skills

Teach study skills and mind mapping. You will find a photocopiable sheet covering these on page 46.

Visual scanning check

If visual scanning is a problem, ask parents or carers to organise an up-to-date eye check for the child, preferably with an orthoptist. Certain orthoptists specialise in Irlen syndrome (a binocular scanning difficulty) and visual dyslexia. They might prescribe a coloured overlay or tinted-spectacle prescription and pupils report that they 'work like magic' and that 'the words stop moving'. There is more information on pages 95 to 96.

Working with challenges
Home help

Harness help from parents and carers, perhaps by teaching them practical approaches and activities. Photocopiable page 47 can be used as a parent take-home when you are asking them to hear their child regularly. Explain to parents which strategy you would like them to use – simple daily reading practice, reading together or paired reading. Photocopiable page 48 contains some games for home for building up short-term memory and phonic skills.

Left-handers

Make sure that writing positions and equipment are appropriate for left-handers. Correct writing and paper position is especially important for left-handed pupils with dyslexia. You will find a useful address of an equipment supplier of left-handed resources on pages 95 to 96.

Mnemonics

Involve the child in working out useful mnemonics for remembering particularly difficult spellings (for example, 'Big elephants can always understand small elephants – 'b' 'e' 'c' 'a' 'u' 's' 'e'.). Collect rhymes and verses that aid spelling rules, such as: '"i" before "e" except after "c".'

Reading recovery

This programme was started in New Zealand and involves a daily individual session. A typical reading recovery lesson includes:

- re-reading a familiar book
- independent reading of a book introduced the previous day
- letter identification using plastic letters

- writing a dictated or prepared story
- sentence building from the story
- introduction of a new book
- guided reading of the new book.

Not surprisingly, the children made very good progress. Good progress is also reported when schools design parent reading schemes and encourage all children and parents to read together each day. There are also various LEA community education schemes to improve parent literacy so that children and parents can improve their skills together.

Teach reversals

By seven, children should have learned to sort out 'b' and 'd' and other reversals. If a child seems 'stuck', teach reversals by designing your own worksheets (see page 31) or making up playing cards with common reversals, such as 'b'/'d'/'p'/'q'. Make it clear where the bottom of the letter is by drawing in a line for the letter to sit on. Use them to play 'Snap', 'Lotto' or 'Pairs'.

Interventions for including children with language difficulties
Working with strengths
Choices

Offer a child with a severe expressive language difficulty choices or alternatives when being asked a question (such as, 'Do you want to finish your story or work on your model?). Illustrations and concrete props can help the development of vocabulary.

Starting points

You need to get to know the child well and to have a clear starting point for your support. Talk with parents and carers. Find out about how much the child understands and how well they can express themselves. How do they make their needs known? Ask parents to tape some language at home (where the child is most relaxed) so that you can have a 'feel' of their stage even if the child says very little in school. Get in touch with any speech and language therapist involved to share assessments and targets.

Visual timetables

You can help a child with language and communication difficulties by showing pictures or symbols about what is going to happen next. Make a series of cards with Velcro backs that can be arranged in line on a felt board. You can also use this to offer choices to a child with little expressive language.

Working with weaknesses
Being patient

Give a child with a language-processing difficulty time to respond or to imitate before you come in with a repetition or the answer. Sometimes the 'Makaton' language programme involving signing can make instructions and requests clearer (see pages 95 to 96).

Change the setting

Some children opt to speak in one situation and not another, this is known as *selective mutism.* These children are often anxious but also determined, and the difficulty can take a few terms to resolve. Be patient and never try to force the child to speak. If at all possible, visit the child at home in order to hear them talk and read there in a relaxed environment. This *changes the setting* of the child's behaviour and develops flexibility. Offer non-verbal ways of responding in class, such as a nod or a hand up at register. Once this is established move on to expecting the child to indicate choices. Ask parents to tape the child's reading at home so that you can monitor progress.

Engaging attention

Children with language and communication difficulties often have poor looking and listening skills. Say their name clearly, get down to their level, try to encourage eye contact albeit briefly (to signal your intent to communicate) and then speak. When you are issuing instructions to the whole class, address the child with difficulties by name first to engage attention. Give very clear and simple messages, showing the child as well as telling them what to do.

Give it time

Some children stammer or stutter and this becomes worse when they are rushed, pressured or feeling self-conscious. Listen patiently to what the child is saying and try not to interrupt. Keep looking at the child as you listen and reply slowly after a second or two's pause. This slows the whole exchange to a more relaxed tempo. Never hurry the child's speech or keep these children from speaking if they are keen to tell you something. If a child has his or her hand up during talking time, let them answer fairly soon to prevent anxiety building up.

Keep it concrete

It is easier to understand what the child is trying to tell you if you are talking about things you have done or shared together. Use props and photographs from home to trigger talk about the child's 'news'. Use real objects to introduce topics. Build in subjects that really interest the child. Relate talk to everyday objects, names and activities in the 'here and now'. Introduce words for objects, actions, smells, colours and textures as you begin new learning activities.

Non-verbal modelling

Children can be *shown* (as well as told) how to sort the concept blocks, organise the puppets for a play or gather data for an experiment. Children with speech and language difficulties sometimes also have difficulties in fine-motor co-ordination and you may need to show the child how to use a pencil or handtool, how to enjoy writing and artwork, and even how to become more personally independent.

Teaching sequences

When you are sharing story books together, spend time discussing the story and predicting what might happen next. Encourage the children to retell the story in their own way, gradually building up to longer sequences. Perhaps at first, for example, a child at Key Stage 1 might predict what is beneath the flap in a familiar 'lift-the-flap' book. In time, they might tell you a whole section of the story and remember what happens at the end as well.

Teach social skills

Identify which behaviour you need to change and decide what new behaviour needs to be taught in its place. Children might need to learn how to make their voices loud or soft when talking and not to shout or whisper all the time. They may need to learn to look at you when speaking or be shown how to greet other children without being too shy or too overwhelming, or how to ask for something rather than grabbing it. Teach the children how to gain attention appropriately with an 'excuse me' rather than a direct interruption.

Tune in to language levels

The best help that you can give the child will be your own language, but delivered at just the right level of complexity or simplicity for the child to understand it and respond to it. Use simple keywords that you have established that the child can understand. Rephrase instructions that have been given to the whole group, keeping them concrete and showing the child what to do as well.

Verbal modelling

For a child with expressive language difficulties, it is helpful for them to hear correct models of what they are trying to say. For example, repeat back, 'Yes, *swallows* fly south *during* the winter', emphasising the word that was mispronounced or the grammatical connecting word that was omitted.

Verbal prompts

When the child is trying to remember a word, you can help by suggesting other clues (for example, 'What did it look like?' or, 'What was it for?') to help the child develop descriptions. Sometimes just providing the initial sound ('It's a g…') can be enough to help them retrieve the word they are searching for.

Working with opportunities

Eye contact

Encourage eye contact by using the child's name, a gentle touch on the shoulder and by speaking at their level, face to face. Praise them for looking at you when you speak to them and also encourage them to look at you when they are speaking to you. Gently point out

that you need to listen to the other children too, using a gentle hand-hold perhaps, to show that you are still 'there' for them while they wait their turn to speak.

Extend imagination
Look for opportunities to help the child think and play imaginatively and to develop symbolic skills. This is especially helpful if the child can learn to play imaginatively with another child. Encourage imaginative thinking and pretend play by basing this on 'real life' experiences such as going to a party together or visiting the supermarket. Miniature play and re-enactions, using small-world resources, can also be helpful and will mean that other children enjoy the learning situation as well.

Facilitate joining in
Use your proximity, your suggestions and your support to make it easier for the child with speech and language difficulties to join in with other children. You might have to interpret what the child is saying to their peers in order to sustain the interaction. Look for ways of making the social learning more enjoyable for everyone.

Peer support
Children whose speech and language development is progressing normally are excellent models for children who have difficulties. Draw attention to children's questions and comments and support the child with difficulties in responding, learning co-operatively or initiating ideas themselves. Start with groups of two children for certain activities and gradually extend the group size.

Play power
You will probably find that the child uses language most fluently during play and free activity times. Try to build these times into the regular day. Look for occasions when you can use language together in a non-direct way, perhaps by talking easily and informally while the child is involved in a creative activity.

Running commentary
Occasionally, work alongside the child with speech and language difficulty and provide a spoken commentary of what they are doing. Don't bombard them with questions, as children with language difficulties do not understand the meaning of question words such as, 'What', 'Why' or 'Which'. Instead, provide simple commentaries and offer choices where possible (for example: 'Do you want the *spiky* one or the *smooth* one?').

Support planning and persistence
Support the children in planning what they are going to do next and help them to see this through, evaluate how it has gone and what they think about it. So, if you are about to make a poster, talk about what it will show and who it will be for. Focus on how you will make it. Then concentrate on how you will display it.

Teach reciprocity

Look for opportunities to encourage the development of turn taking. This important skill leads on to language and conversation later. Simple 'my turn, your turn' activities and board games help this skill to develop. Drama and role-play are excellent ways to develop this and you can also build in many opportunities during circle time.

Time to talk

Encourage conversations by spending quiet moments together and encouraging simple turn taking in what you say, as some children find it hard to learn the 'flow' of speaking first, then listening. Use small-group work to encourage simple conversations with other children, and try to relate them to something concrete that everyone knows about. Encourage the child with disordered language to describe things in an organised way by keeping your commentary well ordered. Who was involved? Where are they? What are they doing? What happened next?

Working with challenges

Double meanings

Children with a language disorder often find it hard to understand double meaning, sarcasm, metaphor or irony. They may interpret it too literally and become confused. Avoid requests such as, 'Would you like to do your writing now?' Replace this with '*Ahmed* – please do your *writing* now.' Make sure that your instructions are concrete, direct and explicit and support these with picture prompts if you need to. Give examples of any double meanings and give an explanation for humour and metaphor if you have to.

Interpretation

For younger children who have difficulty in making their needs known, appoint a key worker at Key Stage 1, such as a learning support assistant, to get to know that child well and to find out about the way they communicate and make their needs known. This key worker will then be able to interpret the child's actions and act on them consistently, thereby ensuring that any signalling of need becomes meaningful and intentional. This person can also put together a 'communication book' (with photographs and descriptions) showing all staff the signs, expressions, words or behaviours that a child uses in order to communicate their feelings and needs.

Reassurance

Ask the staff on duty at break time to stay close by and to be, ready to step in if the child needs support. Children with language difficulties are more likely to lack confidence and feel insecure in a social setting. They might find other children unpredictable or frightening because they have not learned the simple rules of social behaviour or lack words to express themselves. They are likely to feel more confident if a friend or familiar adult is close by to encourage and to reassure.

Picture alphabet

Cut these up and mount them to make a picture alphabet.

How do *you* learn and remember?

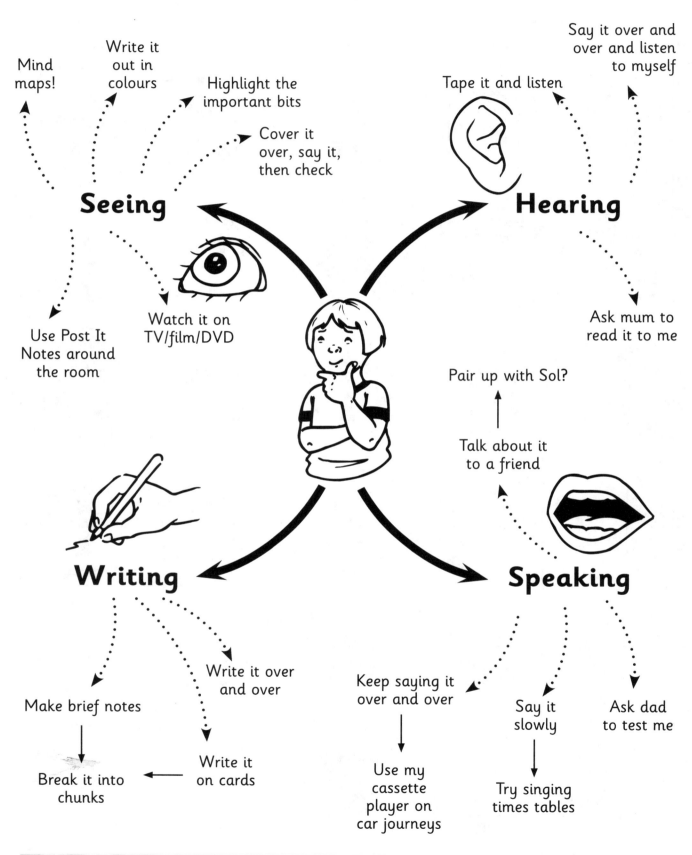

Mind maps!

Write it out in colours

Highlight the important bits

Cover it over, say it, then check

Seeing

Use Post It Notes around the room

Watch it on TV/film/DVD

Say it over and over and listen to myself

Tape it and listen

Hearing

Ask mum to read it to me

Pair up with Sol?

Talk about it to a friend

Writing

Make brief notes

Write it over and over

Break it into chunks

Write it on cards

Speaking

Keep saying it over and over

Use my cassette player on car journeys

Say it slowly

Try singing times tables

Ask dad to test me

Home reading guidelines

Here are some suggestions for supporting your child's reading at home.

Daily reading
- Make sure you are sitting somewhere comfortable, relaxed and quiet.
- Sit close so that you can each see the book.
- Talk about the book first – what has happened so far? Is it a good book?
- Let your child read to you and, if they get stuck, wait for about five seconds before helping.
- Try holding your finger over parts of the word to help your child read individual sounds or chunks.
- Give plenty of praise and encouragement.
- Talk about what you have read afterwards.
- Aim for five minutes per day.

Reading together
- Start by reading a page steadily with your child trying to read at the same time.
- It does not matter if your child does not know each word as you will be saying it for both of you.
- Then repeat the page, but this time stop from time to time for your child to fill in a word independently.
- Try a third time, with your child reading as much as they can without your help.

Paired reading
- Encourage your child to read the words and to nudge you when your help is needed.
- Simply supply the word so that your child can continue reading fluently.

Games to share at home

Here are some ideas for developing your child's memory and listening skills.

I spy
Start with three or four items on a tray and say, for example: 'I spy with my little eye something beginning with "t".' Gradually build up the number of items. Move on to 'I spy with my little eye something ending with "t".' Later, try 'I spy' on long car journeys.

Kim's game
Place three or four items on a tray. Ask your child to look at them for ten seconds. Secretly remove one. Which is missing? Gradually build up the quantity.

Reversals
Make some playing cards out of common reversals such as b/d/p/q. Make it clear where the bottom of the letter is by drawing in a line for the letter to sit on. Use them to play 'Snap'. Adapt them to play 'Lotto' or 'Bingo'. Use them to play 'Pairs'.

Fishing game
Make flashcards of familiar words from the current reading book. Cut them out and add paper clips. Suspend magnets on string to make a fishing game in which your child fishes out the word and names it. Gradually introduce words that look similar and take longer to identify. Use strong rewards and praise. Let your child 'test' you as well as vice versa.

Pencil games
Buy a set of felt-tipped pens. Draw two dots and ask your child to join them. Then take turns drawing two dots for the other to join without crossing any existing lines! You will end up with the paper covered in lines that you have to squeeze between. You can also make patterns with different coloured letters on paper and use it as gift-wrap.

Robot-speak
Speak in letter sounds, rather like a robot, and challenge your child to blend the words together, for example: 'I   a-m   h-u-n-g-r-y.'

Puzzle books
Buy a supply of puzzle books for the holiday and sit down together to encourage and show interest as your child does these.

SPEAKING AND LISTENING

This strand of the National Curriculum will be particularly difficult for pupils with literacy and language difficulties, and will, therefore, provide you with plenty of opportunities for supporting them. Many pupils with dyslexia also have some degree of speech and language difficulty when they are younger and so will be helped by many of the same approaches.

Children with language or literacy difficulties often have poor looking and listening skills, sometimes linked to a poor short-term memory. You will probably find that your best chance of teaching and learning will come through opportunities that arise throughout the school day as you establish starting points and provide running commentary.

You might find that conversational skills need developing by planning activities that teach reciprocity, harness play power and facilitate joining in. Take particular care to explain new vocabulary and to check for understanding as you tune into language levels. Older children will need you to be conscious of and explain double meanings to them and may need your intervention to extend imagination and flexibility of thought. It helps if you can be conscious all the time of the words you are using and how they might be interpreted or misunderstood. For example, children with language difficulties might find it hard to understand humour, metaphor, irony, sarcasm, or figures of speech and idioms, and these might need explanation when you have time to talk.

Throughout the day, you can provide regular reassurance while you speak and listen to each other and use verbal modelling to repeat correctly or to expand what the child has said, keeping this as natural as possible.

When planning a speaking and listening activity for the whole group, think about *engaging attention* first and *being patient* for the child with language difficulties. *Keep it concrete* and use *non-verbal modelling* to make explanations and instructions clear.

Pupils with dyslexia can excel in this strand of the curriculum since written print is not the central purpose. *Encourage oral responses* and use the activities to *build self-esteem* for pupils with dyslexia. If the activity involves an element of reading and writing, look for *alternative means of recording*, *be discreet* and *break steps down* where you have to. If the speaking and listening activity carries a written information sheet or work sheet with it, explore ways of *individualising texts* and make sure you *allow time* for any pupil with dyslexia, language or literacy difficulties to be fully included. Words in italics can be cross referenced to Chapter 3.

AGE RANGE
Five to seven.

GROUP SIZE
Whole group.

LEARNING OBJECTIVE FOR ALL THE CHILDREN
● To act out own and well-known stories, using different voices for characters.

INDIVIDUAL LEARNING TARGET
● To attend to a short story with props and to join in a follow-up activity with confidence.

Whose voice is that?

Children with difficulties in understanding language may find it hard to attend and to listen to stories. Here are some ideas for a story and discussion time that allows you to keep it concrete and facilitate joining in.

What you need
A familiar story or fairy tale, with some repetitive words; simple puppets (enough for one per child).

Preparation
Have ready a simple version of your chosen story. 'The Elves and the Shoemaker', 'Hansel and Gretel', 'Rumpelstiltskin' and 'Cinderella' would all be good choices. Make sure that your version of the story has plenty of speaking parts, and that you have a puppet representation of each character.

What to do
Read the story to the children, using your puppets as props. Use simple and memorable language, making sure that characters have some repeated or predictable words. (For example, the Ugly Sisters might always say, 'Not her!' when Cinderella is mentioned and the Prince might repeat, 'I must find the owner of this shoe', every time it fails to fit.) As you read the story, make changes to your face, manner and voice, matching words to characters.

Discuss the story with the children. Point out that the story would be improved by additional voices. Ask the children if they can help you by speaking the characters' words. Emphasise that scripted lines are not essential – the children just need to say appropriate words. Model this as you read part of the story, and then wait for the children to speak a character's predictable words.

Divide the class into small groups and give out the puppets. Explain, for example, that the group with the Cinderella puppet have become Cinderella so they will say her words.

Read the story, stopping and waiting for the groups to speak their words. Sometimes you may find it easier to select just one Cinderella to speak, though children with difficulties may prefer the security of a group contribution. Make sure that situations recur (for example, the Prince being disappointed that the shoe does not fit) so that words can be repeated.

Special support
Give it time: repeat the story session, so that children with difficulties have the chance to listen and speak with greater certainty. Emphasise keywords and phrases and *tune in to language levels* so that you can *facilitate joining in*.

Extension
Extend the task by giving children new roles. Do they understand this story better now?

AGE RANGE
Five to seven.

GROUP SIZE
Whole group.

LEARNING OBJECTIVE FOR ALL THE CHILDREN
● To secure identification of initial, final and medial letter sounds.

INDIVIDUAL LEARNING TARGET
● To identify an object by its initial sound.

I hear with my little ear...

Children with language and literacy difficulties may find it particularly hard to hear the sounds within words. Here is a concrete and interactive version of 'I spy' that will make phonic learning fun.

What you need
Assortment of objects (or pictures), with familiar names; enough large hoops for the initial and final phonemes used; list of words with selected long-vowel phonemes; individual ✓ cards.

What to do
Give each child an object, asking them to name it. Then place some large hoops on the floor, making the number of hoops match the number of initial sounds used. Place a single object in each hoop, calling out its name and stretching the initial sound ('cccushion'). Ask the children to jump into the hoop which has an object with the same initial phoneme as their object. Are they in the correct hoop?

Put all the objects on a table. Explain that you are going to play a different version of 'I spy' called 'I hear'. Model some examples, giving the children practice in identifying the right object from the initial sound they hear. For example, when you say, 'I hear with my little ear something beginning with "g"', then the children identify and reply, 'golf ball'.

Let the children play the game, taking turns to have the first chance to 'hear' the right object. Divide the class into groups. Children with difficulties may prefer the security of playing the game

within a partnership or small group. Repeat the game using final sounds, then medial sounds. Focus on simple, short-vowel sounds, as in 'ba̱g', 'be̱ll', 'bo̱x', 'cu̱p' and 'bi̱n'. Give each pair of children an object. Call out the middle phoneme you want to hear. Who can hear that sound in the middle of their object's name? Progress to the identification of long-vowel phonemes ('ee', 'ai', 'ie', 'oa', 'oo') as used in the words in NLS Appendix List 3.

Special support
Offer continual *reassurance* to a child with difficulties and *be discreet*, helping the child sound out the name of their object and identify the component sounds before they make use of this information in front of others.

Extension
Play a game in which you write on the board and say the long-vowel phoneme you want to hear. Read the children three words, but say that only one has the matching phoneme. Ask the children, working with partners, to hold up a ✓ card when they hear the object with the correct phoneme.

AGE RANGE
Seven to nine.

GROUP SIZE
Whole group.

LEARNING OBJECTIVE FOR ALL THE CHILDREN
● To improve listening skills.
● To describe and sequence key incidents.

INDIVIDUAL LEARNING TARGET
● To suggest missing words in a spoken story.

Babble gabble

Children with language and literacy difficulties benefit from using meaning and context when retrieving words from their memory. This activity uses an oral cloze procedure to develop that skill.

What you need
Invent some sentences with missing words from a desert island adventure story, for example: 'Friday 13ᵗʰ is always unl_____ (unlucky). The v_____(voyage) started badly. The captain was seas _____(seasick).

Preparation
Prepare a spoken story with details and sequenced events such as:

> Solomon pressed the keys slowly but hard. He was scared of computers. Something always went wrong. Today was no different. He had just written the date – when flash! The screen went blank. He stared, and banged the keys.
> 'Ouch!' said a voice. 'Can't you press gently? I'm not as young as I look. I'm 88 you know.'
> Solomon looked around nervously. Who was whispering to him? Everyone else in the room was typing, with three or four lines done. He started again.
> 'Get off!' screamed the voice. 'I told you – that hurts. Look, stop banging, and I'll do your writing for you. What is it?'
> 'A desert island adventure,' whispered Solomon.

What to do
Read the story, asking the children to try to remember it. Test their memories by playing 'Babble gabble', where they retell the story to a partner as fast as they can but with as much detail as possible. After 20 seconds, you call 'Change!' for the partner to take over. Ask them 'were the details and sequence of events correct?'.

Now the children take turns to be Solomon and dictate a desert island adventure to their partner by playing 'Word tennis', where one child begins to tell the story out loud with a few words before their partner takes over. The storytelling passes between the two children but the sentences and story must make sense.

Next put yourself in Solomon's role. Pretend that your computer left out many of your words. Read out your incomplete sentences, one by one. Can the children help you work out what you said?

Special support
This oral activity allows children who have difficulty with written stories to excel. *Break steps down* and make use of *peer support*.

Extension
The children could invent incomplete sentences for one another.

AGE RANGE
Seven to nine.

GROUP SIZE
Whole group.

LEARNING OBJECTIVE FOR ALL THE CHILDREN
● To present events and characters through dialogue.

INDIVIDUAL LEARNING TARGET
● To interpret non-verbal signals.

Changing places

Children who have had language difficulties when they were younger may still need to develop confidence in speaking out loud.

What you need
List of dramatic school situations: a football comes through a window, a classroom computer falls off its trolley and so on.

Preparation
Select fiction with a number of characters and dramatic scenes. *Harry Potter* by JK Rowling (Bloomsbury), *Alice in Wonderland* by Lewis Carroll, *James and the Giant Peach* by Roald Dahl (Puffin) and *Woof!* by Allan Ahlberg (Puffin) are good possibilities.

What to do
Ask the children to work in pairs. Explain that they have to interpret each other's present mood. Let them guess from *just* facial expressions. Are they right? Extend the work to include body and gesture, but no speaking. Ask partners to show how they felt:
● at lunchtime
● when asked a question during the last lesson
● when they woke up this morning.
Afterwards, encourage the partners to discuss why feelings were (or were not) clear. Was something missing?

Explain to the children that they are now going to use language as well as face and body. Use a credible, but dramatic, school situation: you have lost all your reports! Hold an improvised conversation of about two minutes with your classroom helper about it. Provide the children with some school situations with which they can empathise. Ask partners to choose characters. At a signal from you they must start their improvised dialogue. Signal when to stop, asking the characters to freeze in position. Start again with another situation. Keep the paired improvisation sessions short (about one minute), so that children can build up confidence.

Ask the pairs, in groups of four, to select a familiar, fictional work, and choose an interesting scene. List some of the characters. Allow a few minutes for thinking and planning. Groups can decide ahead the roles (perhaps introducing a new character) and what will happen in two or three minutes of action (perhaps different from the book). Do <u>not</u> decide what characters will say in advance.

Special support
Be aware of children whose confidence is still fragile and provide *reassurance*. Move among pairs, supporting children in difficulty.

Extension
Consider repeat performances for an audience of yourself, another group of four or the whole class.

AGE RANGE
Nine to eleven.

GROUP SIZE
Whole group.

LEARNING OBJECTIVE FOR ALL THE CHILDREN
● To investigate words which have common letter strings.

INDIVIDUAL LEARNING TARGET
● To identify and manipulate letter sounds within a spoken word.

Sound detectives

Children with dyslexia often find it hard to hear the sounds within words. Here are some ideas for teaching *phonological awareness*.

What you need
Selection of phrases in which you have interchanged sounds; tape recorder and tape recording for each group of four children; facilities for recording the children's words.

Preparation
Make a tape of confused speech. For example: 'Open bour yooks. *(your books)* Kool at nage pen. *(Look, page, ten)* Dook lown to the cight rorner. *(Look, down, right, corner)* Cat wholour is it? *(What colour)* Dou yon't mees to know? *(You, don't, seem)* I can't erndustand. *(understand)* This is no doog. *(good)* You are not hying trard enough. *(trying hard)* KOOL! *(Look).*'

What to do
Set the following scenario. You have a new teacher who is an alien. She has tried to learn English but her speech has got muddled up! She keeps putting sounds in the wrong order. The result is gibberish! Let the children collaborate in pairs or groups of three, trying to make sense of what you read out. Keep the exercise fun. Here are some examples (translated to help you with pronunciation):

> Chop statting. (*Stop chatting*) Dit soun. (*Sit down*) Bet your gooks. (*Get your books*) Han you cear? (*Can you hear?*) Ge bood! (*Be good!*) Lestin! (*Listen!*)

Write some examples on the board and analyse what the alien teacher was saying. Ask the children, in pairs, to give their partner a short instruction. Can the partner turn the words into gibberish?

Next, one child gives a gibberish instruction and the partner has a minute to guess its meaning. Explain that you have made a tape of more of the alien teacher's lesson. The children have to be sound detectives. Put the children into groups of about four. Provide tapes and listening space. Ask them to listen to the tape, identify errors, translate them into real English and make a new, correct tape.

Special support
If some children seem confused, *give it time* – slow down and explain some examples in detail. Provide magnetic letters as a visual aid.

Extension
Talk about Spoonerisms and see whether the children can include these within a nonsense poem.

AGE RANGE
Nine to eleven.

GROUP SIZE
Whole group.

LEARNING OBJECTIVE FOR ALL THE CHILDREN
● To perform poems in a variety of ways.
● To listen to and evaluate performances of poems.

INDIVIDUAL LEARNING TARGET
● To demonstrate the use of rhyme and rhythm when speaking.

Rhythm and rhyme

Children with dyslexia or language difficulties usually benefit from practice in hearing rhyming sounds and gaining a feel for the rhythm of language.

What you need
Individual copies of photocopiable page 56.

What to do
Look together at the poem 'Leisure Centre, Pleasure Centre'. Read it to and with the children. Point out how the poem comes alive when read aloud. Why is this? (Oral performance draws attention to the rhymes and rhythm.) Point out how the short lines in the poem give speed to the rhythm helping the audience to enjoy the treats of the leisure centre.

Divide the poem into halves. Put the children into groups of four and ask them to prepare a performance of half the poem. Ask them to consider:
● presentation style
● matching tone with meaning
● making rhymes obvious
● bringing out rhythm
● choosing volume
● using a balance of voices (not everyone has to speak at once).

Allow ten minutes for group discussion. Then ask each group to link up with a group that has prepared the other half of the poem. Give ten minutes for rehearsals by the new, larger groups. Then let the children perform for and listen to one another.

Now the children should be ready to write their own poems. Investigate the structure of the 'Leisure Centre' poem. Point out the longer lines used to introduce and finish and remind the children of the emphasis on rhyme and fast rhythm.

Ask the children in small groups to use the supplied opening and finishing lines (see photocopiable page 56). They need to write short rhyming couplets listing the treats on a seaside trip. Consider useful verbs ('lie', 'loll', 'bask', 'dig', 'build', 'play', 'burrow', 'run', 'swim', 'splash', 'paddle'). Encourage the groups to work in rough; to be willing to change words as they think of better alternatives; to read lines aloud to each other to check the rhythm. Set a time limit of about 20 minutes. Compare progress.

Special support
Be discreet: use the working time to offer support and *reassurance* to children with difficulties. *Break steps down* for children with language difficulties who may need extra help with *double meanings*, abstract language and subtle turns of phrase.

Extension
Hold a performance poetry festival and let the children enjoy one another's results.

Poems with rhythm and rhyme

Leisure Centre, Pleasure Centre
(extract)

A leisure centre trip is the best of treats because you can

keep fit

leap sit

eat crisps

do twists

belly flop

pit stop

fill up

with 7-Up

get going

blood flowing

look snappy

be happy

in the leisure centre, pleasure centre.

John Rice (from *The Works* by Paul Cookson, Macmillan Children's Books)

A Seaside Trip

A seaside trip is the best of treats because you can

_____

_____

_____

_____

_____

_____

_____

_____

_____

_____

_____

_____

at the beach side, seaside.

Eileen Jones (based on 'Leisure Centre, Pleasure Centre' by John Rice)

SPECIAL NEEDS **in the primary years: Dyslexia and language difficulties**

READING

This strand of the curriculum has been chosen because of the difficulty that it poses for children with dyslexia. Even if a child has received specialist support in the past and has now developed a single-word reading age more or less in line with the age or ability, there are likely to be subtle and persistent difficulties for them in reading texts fluently and quickly for meaning. This is one of the reasons why examination concessions or additional time become so important later on – it allows these children the chance to show examiners their cognitive worth. You will probably find that children with dyslexia need you to allow time which is longer than usual so that they can read and re-read any written material – once to crack the words and at least once more to derive meaning from the passage.

Encourage children with dyslexia to make use of highlighting to make written facts easier to digest. Consider presenting written material in different forms: mind maps, individualised texts and making use of clever colours.

You may need to work more closely on their phonological awareness or on their use of context using cloze procedure, perhaps through small-group tuition in which you plan structured, multi-sensory and cumulative teaching. For pupils at Key Stage 1, pictograms and teaching reversals will help develop confidence when sounding new words out and you will find it vital to harness home help as far as possible. You will find a photocopiable parent sheet on page 47 for supporting reading skills at home.

Sometimes you will need to arrange a period of consistent reading recovery in order to improve basic reading skills, perhaps working in conjunction with a learning support teacher or dyslexia specialist.

For children with a language difficulty, learning to read can actually help them make sense of grammatical order and tenses. If they have a speech difficulty, you might find that they are mispronouncing words even when reading and you can use verbal modelling to repeat back phrases correctly. Be discreet and do not ask a child with a language or literacy difficulty to read aloud in front of others unless they are keen to. Remember to test for comprehension regularly by tuning into language levels. Teach double meanings and use written text to extend imagination, making sure that you have time to talk together about the passages.

AGE RANGE
Five to seven.

GROUP SIZE
Small group.

LEARNING OBJECTIVE FOR ALL THE CHILDREN
● To practise and secure phonic knowledge.
● To secure reading of initial letter sounds.

INDIVIDUAL LEARNING TARGET
● To learn single letter sounds.

Who am I?

Children with language and literacy difficulties usually find it easiest to learn letters in a multi-sensory way. Here is an activity for helping them learn letter sounds.

What you need
Copies of the 'Picture alphabet' on photocopiable page 45.

Preparation
Use an earlier session for the children to make and cut out the letters from photocopiable page 45. The children will find this easy, but tell them their letters are going to prove very useful. Collect the letters up ready for the game.

What to do
Remind the children about the 'Picture alphabet' they coloured and cut out in a previous session. Explain that they are now going to play a game of 'Who am I?' Shuffle and deal about six letter cards to each of them. Tell the children that they have to keep their cards unseen by anyone else.

Ask the children to take turns to play, using one of their cards. Will the other children guess the card's identity? Clues are given by saying the sound shown. For example, for a 'w' letter card with a picture of a worm, a child might say: 'I start with "w", and I wriggle. Who am I?'

Let the children take turns. Who is good at guessing? Who gives clever and correct clues? Tell the children that you are keeping a secret score. Play a few rounds of the game, shuffling and re-dealing the cards, so that everyone gains experience of handling, looking at, and reading different letters. At the end of the game, you could make some awards.

Special support
This is a motivating way to help children develop phonological awareness. If you think some children are experiencing difficulties, let them work with partners. Allow time and make sure that weaker children have a chance to guess. Presenting awards is a useful way to boost the confidence and build self-esteem of children who usually experience reading difficulties.

Extension
Play an extended version of the game to develop skills further. Put the cards face down on the table. Each child picks a card in turn. Can the child make up a correct 'Who am I?' clue to fit the letter, but not to fit the picture? Now the children have more to do: they have to identify the letter sound and they have to relate it to another word. For example, for the 'w' card, a child could say: 'I start with the letter "w", and I tell the time' (a watch). Again, play the game a few times to develop the children's confidence and to provide them all with the opportunity to both set clues and answer the puzzle.

AGE RANGE
Five to seven.

GROUP SIZE
Whole group.

LEARNING OBJECTIVE FOR ALL THE CHILDREN
● To learn spellings of verbs with '-ing' (present tense) endings.

INDIVIDUAL LEARNING TARGET
● To read and use simple action words – 'running', 'sitting', 'standing' and so on.

Stay sensible!

Children with language difficulties will need extra practice in vocabulary and grammatical constructions such as action words.

What you need
'Yes' and 'No' cards for each child; questions on large, separate pieces of card; cards with simple sentences, using present tense action verbs ('-ing' endings).

Preparation
Write questions on card for your game of 'Sensible questions'. Make your 'action' cards. Ensure the writing is large enough for the children to read. Decide on an area where the children will have space for movement.

What to do
Tell the children that you have a new problem: you sometimes start being silly. In fact, it has happened today, but only when you were with the teachers! Now you are worried that it could start happening when you are teaching the children.

Explain that you want to practise reading verbs in a game called 'Sensible questions'. You will hold up a question on a big card. The children will have answer cards – 'Yes' and 'No' – and they must hold up the correct one. Give the children some examples, 'Can a man run?', 'Has a spider got four legs?'

Play the game, making sure that all children have time to show their answer cards. Try to include some questions to which both 'Yes' and 'No' are correct (for example, 'Can you skip?'). Question the children about their answers to check that they understand the question. Slip in some silly questions. Do the children spot them?

Now give the children more space. Tell them that you are going to shut your eyes and just hold up a card, saying an action they should do. How many will be doing the right action when you open your eyes? Hold up cards with present tense '-ing' forms of verbs on them, for example 'You are hopping'. Make sure that you slip in a few silly instructions! such as 'Everyone is pulling a face'!

Special support
You may want to put some children with a partner for support.

Extension
Try varying the game, so that only part of the class is doing the actions, while the rest takes turns, with partners, holding up the cards. The partners need to work out what the card says.

AGE RANGE
Seven to nine.

GROUP SIZE
Whole group.

LEARNING OBJECTIVE FOR ALL THE CHILDREN
● To read and follow simple instructions.

INDIVIDUAL LEARNING TARGET
● To read and act upon simple written instructions.

Instructions

Children with reading difficulties may need more than the usual encouragement and motivation. This activity makes a simple spelling task fun.

What you need
Individual copies of a text, and clues to identifiy specific words.

Preparation
Make up a text containing about 15 spellings which you want the children to learn for homework. Write instructions which will lead the children to the words. The example below uses and underlines compound words from NLS Spelling Bank pages 12 and 13. You could then choose two or three other words containing silent letters.

What a morning! <u>Everything</u> has gone wrong. First of all I was suffering with a raging <u>headache</u>. I knew that my fridge and cupboard would be empty after the <u>weekend</u>, so I had nothing to eat for <u>breakfast</u>. Then <u>someone</u> rang, just as I was planning to leave, so that made me late. In fact, there was <u>nobody</u> on the phone: it was <u>somebody</u> fooling around. At school there was <u>nowhere</u> to park. In the end, the <u>headteacher</u> came out and shouted, 'Leave your wreck <u>anywhere</u>!'

By the time I walked across the <u>playground</u>, the <u>headteacher</u> was in my <u>classroom</u>, writing something on the <u>blackboard</u>. I just knew that meant extra trouble for me.

Sample instructions could follow this form:
● Use the fourth word of my story. (everything)
● Look for the place the headteacher shouted about. (anywhere)
● Pick the word with eight letters on the second line. (headache)

What to do
Explain to the children that this week's spelling list has a difference: they have to find out for themselves what the words are. All they have to do is read the passage and then read and follow the instructions. Give out copies of your text and instructions. Tell the children the number of words they will be listing. Suggest that they write the words on paper before entering them in their homework books.

Special support
Provide highlighting pens to help some children engage attention and keep their place.

Extension
Reverse the activity: provide a list of spellings for the children to build into a short story.

AGE RANGE
Seven to nine.

GROUP SIZE
Whole group.

LEARNING OBJECTIVE FOR ALL THE CHILDREN
● To identify the main characteristics of key characters, using them to write character sketches.

INDIVIDUAL LEARNING TARGET
● To recognise the link between a mind map and the facts in a written text.

Mind-reading

Mind maps **can be a powerful tool for children with literacy difficulties to plot their ideas.**

What you need
Copies of photocopiable page 64.

Preparation
Ensure that you are familiar with mind maps – you may wish to read Mind Maps for Kids by Tony Buzan (Harper Collins). Make individual copies of photocopiable page 64.

What to do
Set a scenario:

> Eric, a famous writer, is ready to describe a key character in his book. Unfortunately, he has forgotten the ideas he had; all he has left is a rather strange diagram that he once made. What does it mean?

Look at photocopiable page 64. Can the children understand it? Allow five to ten minutes of partner discussion and then talk about the page as a whole class. The children should be able to work out that the author has made a character sketch in note form. What are Matt's main likes? How many are there? What do the shorter branches mean? Explain that this link could be emphasised by using the same colour. Point out that letter size indicates the relative importance of words. Discuss the usefulness of the pictures. Explain that this is a mind map and can be a very useful way of recording early thoughts about a subject.

Now the children are to become Eric: they are to finish off the mind map for Matt's dislikes. Encourage them to finalise their choices of words on a rough version before using the proper map. Compare finished maps, asking children to 'read' aloud from them (to a partner if some children prefer). Reading should be in sentences, not just the single words on their maps.

Special support
Trying a rough draft first will give confidence to children who need spelling support. Mind maps help children with reading difficulties to be more fluent when they have recorded in this way. Teach study skills by showing children how to make use of mind maps when planning, revising and remembering.

Extension
Ask the children to now continue to role-play Eric, and write a description of the character Matt Wordy. Remind them to make sure that the description fits the mind map.

AGE RANGE
Nine to eleven.

GROUP SIZE
Whole group.

LEARNING OBJECTIVE FOR ALL THE CHILDREN
● To evaluate their work.

INDIVIDUAL LEARNING TARGET
● To design and print an information sheet that is personally easy to decipher.

Read this!

Children with dyslexia have very individual preferences for font size, spacing, colouring and type when they are reading. This activity has pupils experimenting with *using ICT* and texts.

What you need
OHP slide of your handwritten, difficult-to-read teaching instructions for a supply teacher; science text book.

Preparation
Type and save a piece of science information about the benefits of a varied diet. (The need for fruit and vegetables, the need to avoid too much sugar and the need for balance.) Deliberately use smaller font, closer spacing and a poorer layout than the children are used to. Do not use colours, bold font, new paragraphs or headings or anything that helps display the text. Make the file accessible on the children's computers ready for the activity.

What to do
Explain to the children that you have been asked to improve the layout and appearance of a piece of writing so that it is easier to understand. Use an OHP display of the scribbled notes that you have made for your lesson plans. You want to leave them for a supply teacher, but the headteacher cannot understand them. What are the children's comments?

Model some improvements to the notes but point out that a computer would make the writing clearer. Discuss the benefits of a computer-generated text (clear letters, underlining and highlighting; a font that suits the reader; the choice of line and word spacing).

Show the children a text in a science book aimed at their age group. Identify how the writer uses these various means to make sure that the words are comfortable to read and the information is therefore accessible.

Ask the children to work in pairs – this will be helpful for children who have reading difficulties. Explain that you have saved a text for them but they may find it difficult to read. Can they improve it? Encourage them to say if they find a particular font difficult. Give them time to experiment with font and layout. Print and display the results. Which one gets the vote for the most reader-friendly page?

Special support
Emphasise the usefulness of ICT, highlighting and individualised texts. Ask the children with difficulties what methods work best for them and make use of this information when preparing written texts for them.

Extension
Use what you have learned about the effective use of clear fonts and well designed layout to design school pamphlets and guidelines.

AGE RANGE
Nine to eleven.

GROUP SIZE
Whole group, in pairs.

LEARNING OBJECTIVE FOR ALL THE CHILDREN
● To look at connections and contrasts in the work of different writers.

INDIVIDUAL LEARNING TARGET
● To enjoy reading chosen books with a partner.

Bookworms

Make use of peer support for developing confidence and practice when reading. Here are some ideas.

What you need
Novels and short stories for the children to choose from.

Preparation
Ask the children to bring one or two favourite fiction texts, from home or school. You may decide to focus on books of one genre. Ask them to write down why they like the books and to choose an extract which they think shows why the book is worth reading.

What to do
Explain your objective: to recommend reading books to the children in another upper-junior class. You plan to publish 'The Reading News' but you need book reviews from the children.

Ask the children to work with partners; their partners will be their reading buddies. Talk about what the children should discuss (content, style, audience appeal). Collect and list a selection of conversation starters: do this by considering possible questions the reading buddies can ask each other. Suggest that partners begin their discussion by reading an extract to each other. Then they must explain why they think this writing is effective. What are its special strengths? Does the extract have any weaknesses? How does it compare with the reading buddy's selection?

Explain that 'The Reading News' will only have space for one recommendation between the two of them. Which book is it to be? Ask them to list the strengths and weaknesses of their choices. Which book scores best? List what upper-junior readers might be looking for in a book they read. Which book meets most of the needs? Emphasise that partners must reach a joint view.

Read some examples of book reviews in magazines. (Junior Education magazine (Scholastic) always carries a selection.) Explain the purpose of a review (to give a flavour of the book and to make it clear if it is likely to suit you). Suggest they write about 100–130 words. Let the children use computers to write their book reviews so they can take turns at writing it.

Special support
Children with reading difficulties will benefit from the support of a more confident buddy. Break steps down where needed and be ready to support struggling partnerships.

Extension
Now you must publish! Put together an editorial team and make sure that they seek feedback from the whole class from time to time.

Eric's new book

This activity is based on the ideas in *Mind Maps for Kids* by Tony Buzan (Thorsons, 2003).

SPECIAL NEEDS in the primary years: Dyslexia and language difficulties

WRITING

This strand of the curriculum has been included because of the challenges it poses to children with dyslexia. Children with language difficulties should manage on the whole with your usual approaches. Most children who have a specific learning difficulty affecting their reading will also have difficulties with spelling and many may also find that handwriting does not flow smoothly for them as a means of recording.

At Key Stage 2, it is often a child's writing that first alerts you to a specific learning difficulty and, on closer inspection, you might find that the accuracy, speed or comprehension of reading are also affected. While handwriting and spelling will certainly need additional support, try to do this as a separate exercise from the day-to-day work that the child is doing in class. Otherwise, a feeling of failure can pervade every area of learning.

The child may be having additional small-group or individual tuition to support their learning difficulty. If so, try to liaise with the tutor so that you can focus in class on the words that the child has learned in tutorials and help the child to generalise spellings in their daily work. That way, you will be marking written work for just a few targeted spellings and then focusing on content rather than accuracy. Ask the tutor in advance to cover certain vocabulary and spellings necessary for your next topic work in class so that the child with dyslexia is well prepared.

Make use of *alternative means of recording* and *encourage oral responses* to ensure that a child with dyslexia feels successful and has a chance to excel and to *build self-esteem*. Teach keyboard skills and use *ICT* at the earliest opportunity, in parallel to the *structured, multi-sensory and cumulative teaching*

that you may be providing for spelling and writing skills. Take time to *break steps down* before any writing activity and encourage the child to approach you for support between each step. It can be helpful if you bring on board *home help* and teach parents or carers how to use *mnemonics* and the *SOS technique* for learning spellings or corrections. For children at Key Stage 1, check writing position and letter formation before bad habits are formed and make sure that you make provision for *left-handers*. By the middle of Key Stage 2, you might feel that a child would benefit from *spelling aids,* which can assist memory and learning by providing more clues.

AGE RANGE
Five to seven.

GROUP SIZE
Whole group.

LEARNING OBJECTIVE FOR ALL THE CHILDREN
● To form lower-case letters correctly.
● To secure the ability to hear initial phonemes in CVC words.
● To read on sight familiar words.

INDIVIDUAL LEARNING TARGET
● To form letters correctly.

Help Teddy

Learning correct letter formation must be mastered at this stage before bad habits are formed. Here is an activity that makes it fun and inspires success.

What you need
Six postcard-size pieces of card per child; a favourite class teddy or other stuffed toy to use as a prop.

Preparation
Prepare a bank of appropriate CVC words.

What to do
Revise lower-case letters with the class, demonstrating how each one is written, putting particular emphasis on the correct starting points. Let the children repeat your letter formation by tracing the letter shapes in the air. Make sure that the children have plenty of space, and they can see and be seen by you so that faults are put right.

Tell the children that writing and reading are connected: a letter that looks wrong is not easy to understand. Use the favourite class teddy. Explain that Teddy is having problems with his reading and writing as he is always forgetting his starting letter. Will they be able to help? Ask them to make labels – word and picture – to help him learn. Stress the need for good writing and letters formed correctly.

Provide a list of 20 three-letter words, each with the initial letter missing. Beside each word, put two letters (both of which would fit in the gap) and a rudimentary picture. The children have to decide which letter begins the word for your picture, for example, m/ran; d/log; b/red; t/din; b/dig; b/rag; s/fun; l/day; d/cot; b/mat.

Now ask the children to use the unused initial letters to make new words, supplying their own pictures. Let them each choose six of the 20 words and make picture word cards for Teddy. The cards can be kept in a dictionary pile next to him and used as a teaching resource when a human friend reads them to him and demonstrates how to write the letters.

Special support
Make use of *clever colours* to highlight different letters or beginnings and endings. If necessary, make time to *teach reversals.* The use of Teddy should help to *engage attention* and *keep it concrete* for children with language difficulties.

Extension
Add CCVC, CVCC and irregular words to the dictionary pile as Teddy becomes more competent!

AGE RANGE
Five to seven.

GROUP SIZE
Whole class.

LEARNING OBJECTIVE FOR ALL THE CHILDREN
● To write and re-read own sentences for sense, spelling and punctuation.

INDIVIDUAL LEARNING TARGET
● To construct a simple sentence from word cards and copy it into a book.

Write away!

Children who struggle with handwriting may benefit from alternative approaches to sentence building enabling them to copy.

What you need
Small pieces of card for the children to write separate words on – about 12 pieces of card per child; pieces of paper (A4 or A3) which can be joined together to form a book; pens and felt-tipped pens.

Preparation
Select a picture storybook with only a small amount of text – perhaps a single sentence on each page. Decide on a title for the book to be written by the children.

What to do
Show the children your picture storybook. Demonstrate how the illustrations and text support and add to each other. Emphasise that the text consists of proper sentences.

Now point out the name of the author. State your objective: to produce a book with many authors – namely, the whole class. Explain that everybody will write and illustrate one page of the book. Agree that the book will go in your reading corner, or be put on display for parents, so you want it to be as good as possible.

Tell the children that the book's title will be, for example, 'Funny Dreams'. They can write about real or imaginary dreams. Model an example sentence: 'I waved my magic wand and the noisy children went to sleep.'

Next ask the children for their ideas. Set a guide for the length of sentences (about six to 12 words). Ask the children to decide on and then write their sentences, putting each word on a separate piece of card. You or your helper should check everyone's spelling and punctuation.

Now the children must put their cards face down on the table and jumble them up. When they turn them over, can they re-form their sentence? Check that the sentence is correct before it is copied on to the special paper for the story book. Ask the children to add their illustrations.

You may decide to ask all the children to make sample book covers – and choose the best. When you are ready to put the book together, consider laminating the pages and cover.

Special support
Some children may need to dictate their words to you or your helper. Cut them up on to separate cards and support the child's *sequencing skills* as these are reassembled.

Extension
Make up a group story and write each sentence on a card for older children to reassemble and write out.

AGE RANGE
Seven to nine.

GROUP SIZE
Whole group.

LEARNING OBJECTIVE FOR ALL THE CHILDREN
● To use spelling strategies, and to investigate and use the spelling pattern '-le'

INDIVIDUAL LEARNING TARGET
● To hear and record the sounds within words.

Listen and look

Children who find it hard to hear the sounds within words are particularly challenged by spelling. Here are some ideas for teaching phonological awareness.

What you need
Individual whiteboards or 'show me' cards.

Preparation
Collect word banks for spelling and rhyming examples.

What to do
Tell the children that they are going to use their eyes and ears to become better spellers. Begin with a game of 'Odd man out'. This is an oral game, in which you say groups of words and the children tell you the word that does not rhyme with the rest (for example, 'cat', 'rat', '<u>cart</u>', 'chat'; 'dinner', 'winner', '<u>runner</u>'; 'write', '<u>wrote</u>', 'fright', 'fight', 'slight'.) Provide plenty of quick practice. Finish with some words ending in '-le' (riddle, '<u>silly</u>', 'wriggle', 'sizzle', 'bubble').

Then display these words: 'riddle', 'wriggle', 'waffle', 'bubble'. Point out the '-le' spelling pattern and discuss the sound produced. Investigate the words. Can the children identify another common spelling feature? (Double letters before '-le'.) Ask the children what do they notice about the appearance and shape of the letters just before '-le'? (Preceding letters often have an ascender or descender.) Practise spelling other words which follow this rule ('rubble', 'kettle', 'ripple'), using 'show me' techniques as the children hold up the written spelling of your oral word.

Show about ten word beginnings: 'han-', 'chu-', 'c-', 'noo-', 'ici-', 'relia-', 'obsta-', 'pi-', 'grum-', 'cubi-'. Now display the following '-le' word endings as family group headings: '-ckle' (chuckle); '-able' (fable); '-dle' (candle); '-ble' (trouble), and '-cle' (miracle). Ask the children to match a beginning to a family-group heading to make a word.

Next the children should think of their own word beginnings in order to extend their lists, aiming at perhaps six words in each family group. Stress that family members must rhyme with one another and must end with their correct letters.

Share the results, encouraging the children to use eyes and ears to spot words that look or sound wrong.

Special support
Less confident children may benefit from working with partners. With some children you may need to *keep it concrete* by offering context clues or provide *verbal prompts* such as word beginnings.

Extension
If there is time, extend this activity by adding '-ible' and '-ple' to your family groups. Encourage the children to find appropriate word beginnings to match these endings.

AGE RANGE
Seven to nine.

GROUP SIZE
Whole group.

LEARNING OBJECTIVE FOR ALL THE CHILDREN
● To identify misspelled words in own writing.

INDIVIDUAL LEARNING TARGET
● To identify and correct their own spelling mistakes.

Spot the mistakes!

Children lose confidence when their work is continually corrected but they need to improve their spelling. This challenging activity will help.

What you need
Paper; pen; individual whiteboards or 'show me' cards.

Preparation
Write a silly paragraph of text covering spelling rules that you want to teach. Have a copy ready to give to every child.

What to do
Dictate the paragraph of text to the children to write down:

> He was so greedy he grabbed the lot! For one dinner, he had four pieces of plaice in batter, a whole cake with a cherry on, ice cream and two apples. To make him stop eating, he had to be dragged away from the table. 'What is there for supper?' he cried.

Ask the children to put this writing aside. Now hand out the correct version of the text to each child and consider some of the spelling rules just used. For example, long vowels in the middle of words are followed by a single consonant – 'cake', 'make'; but short vowels are followed by two consonants – 'dinner', 'cherry'. Thought-storm topic or family words with double letters after short vowels. Use them in oral sentences, asking the children to display the correct spelling on 'show me' cards or individual whiteboards. Ask them to return to their writing and focus on those rules.

Now play 'Word sums', in which you add '-ed' to verbs, for example, 'drop' + '-ed' = 'dropped'. Include verbs ending in '-y', for example, 'try' + '-ed' = 'tried'. Provide plenty of practice. Play 'Confusion': write a sentence, missing out a word, and tell the children common homophones that are confusing you. Can they write the correct one for you? Useful homophones include: 'there', 'their' and 'they're'; 'two', 'to' and 'too'; 'for' and 'four'; 'whole' and 'hole'. Let the children look again at their writing. Do they want to make more corrections? Can they identify their own errors?

Special support
Weaker children may be happier working in pairs – let partners help each other when necessary. *Break steps down* and use *SOS* to teach new spellings. Weak spellers may find *mnemonics* useful: 'Number four needs four letters'.

Extension
Move on to letting the children work with partners, giving each other sentences to write, trying to use rules looked at in the lesson.

AGE RANGE
Nine to eleven.

GROUP SIZE
Whole group.

LEARNING OBJECTIVE FOR ALL THE CHILDREN
● To write a poem, making careful choice of words and phrases.

INDIVIDUAL LEARNING TARGET
● To prepare a short piece of written work on computer for display.

Extraordinary words

Using computers allows children with dyslexia to produce accurate and neat work that they can feel proud of and so free up their creativity.

What you need
Individual copies of page 72; computers; large bag of everyday objects, such as a mobile phone, pen, diary, mirror.

Preparation
Prepare similes and metaphors to describe your bag's contents.

What to do
Explain that you need extraordinary words for ordinary objects. As you display your bag's contents, make imaginative comparisons, 'My biro is like a striped stick of rock'. Encourage the children's suggestions. Do they recognise the descriptions as similes? Ask the children which word identifies the simile (like). Continue with your props, but using metaphors: 'My pen is a striped stick of rock' or 'My mirror is a calm pond'. Explain that, with a metaphor, you are no longer saying that your mirror is *like* a pond; you are saying it *is* a pond. Ask the children for examples. Find other examples from the poem 'My Literacy Book' on photocopiable page 72.

Challenge the children to write, as poems, imaginative descriptions of school objects or places. Stress how poems vary – both in structure and style.

Ask the children to choose subjects, for example: the computer, interactive whiteboard, television, chair, dining hall, wall bars, football pitch. Suggest jotting down words, phrases, similes and metaphors in rough, gradually drafting lines. Stress that rhyme is not

essential. Mention layout explain that using the computer will offer more freedom with visual presentation. Talk about linking text design with meaning. For example, a poem about a table might have four words, written vertically, representing the legs. Show the them the poem 'Undersea Tea' on the photocopiable sheet. Use the computers, for writing, editing and revising. Plan time for sharing the poems.

Special support
Build self-esteem by suggesting reading lines aloud to a response partner, encouraging evaluation. *Individualise text* as enlarged font can help children who have reading problems. *Encourage oral responses* as a first step. Explain *double meanings*.

Extension
Encourage children to create, write and print anthologies of their work.

AGE RANGE
Nine to eleven.

GROUP SIZE
Whole group.

LEARNING OBJECTIVE FOR ALL THE CHILDREN
● To identify misspelled words; to apply knowledge of spelling rules, and to use dictionaries and IT Spell Checks.

INDIVIDUAL LEARNING TARGET
● To select the correct spelling from a Spell-Check menu.

Write the right word

The use of Spell Check on the computer can actually improve spelling rather than replace it for a child with dyslexia.

What you need
Dictionaries; computers with Spell Check (one for each child, if possible); a prepared newspaper article with spelling mistakes.

Preparation
Type and print individual copies of a text with spelling mistakes. Make errors a mixture of non-existent words and incorrect word selections, some typical of the children's mistakes. For example:

> It was a grat book – I juste wish it had more pages. The begining was exiting fou peepl hoo enjoy fantasy, because the wrightr went srait intwo tieme travel. The buoye was uusing his computer whn alowd noise sownded and a lite dassled hm. It was actially coming from hiz tellevission. Their was something rong! A gurl appiered on the screan, stepped out, and… Reede the buk two fined out wat happens nexxed.

What to do
Explain your objective: to improve spelling skills. After a brief revision of computer Spell Checks and dictionaries, distribute copies of your prepared text. Say that this is a journalist's rushed copy. The children, as newspaper editors, must correct it. Ask them to underline, by hand, words which look incorrect. Then ask the children to type out the text exactly as it was given to them. Does the Spell Check highlight the words that they underlined?

Allow 15 minutes for the 'editors' to make corrections. Compare results. Which words were hardest to identify? Did the Spell Check fail to identify errors? Point out that if words exist, but are used incorrectly, Spell Checks may not help. List strategies used to identify mistakes, for example, visual skills, checking how words look, meanings, context and spelling patterns.

Special support
Break steps down by offering this sentence by sentence. *Individualise text* by using larger font and highlighting errors you wish to draw to the child's attention. Offer limited *choices* as a way of making this activity simpler so that you can *build self-esteem*.

Extension
Encourage some of the children to practise their new editing skills by working together to write and compile a class newsletter. Suggest that the children take it in turns to write and correct each others' text, and print out the final result.

Extraordinary poems

My Literacy Book

The empty page is a field of snow,

Fresh, clean, unmarked, empty.

It awaits my footprints;

Yet still I hover on the edge,

Reluctant to blot its glaring beauty.

With a sigh, I grasp my walking stick,

And begin to plot my route,

Marking a track from one side to the other.

Eileen Jones

Undersea Tea

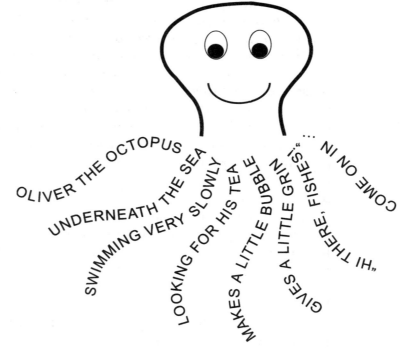

OLIVER THE OCTOPUS
UNDERNEATH THE SEA
SWIMMING VERY SLOWLY
LOOKING FOR HIS TEA
MAKES A LITTLE BUBBLE
GIVES A LITTLE GRIN
"HI THERE, FISHES" ...
COME ON IN

Tony Mitton (from *The Works* by Paul Cookson, Macmillan Children's Books)

NUMBER AND ALGEBRA

There is an overlap between specific literacy difficulties and specific numeracy difficulties and you might well find that a child has difficulties in mathematics as well as in reading, spelling or writing. The same short-term working memory that contributes to a weakness in reading and spelling may also lead to a weakness in recalling times tables or simple number bonds. A difficulty in remembering reversals and in spatial processing can lead to problems in setting out calculations. After all, although we write from left to right, we actually calculate with hundreds, tens and units from right to left, and this can easily confuse some children. This strand of the curriculum has been included because of the challenges it can pose to children with specific learning difficulties such as dyslexia. Consider the use of *small-group tuition*, *musical sequences* and *home help* to overcome any developing problems as early as possible.

Children with language difficulties can also find aspects of numberwork difficult. You might suppose that a child is struggling with handling the mathematics, whereas in fact they have misunderstood the problem. At Key Stage 1, errors might arise through a misunderstanding of the basic mathematical vocabulary, such as 'plus', 'minus', 'more than', 'less than', 'over', 'greater' and 'same as'. Many of the words we use in mathematics carry identical meanings such as 'add', 'sum' and 'plus'; 'share' and 'divide', and 'multiply' and 'times'. *Tune into language levels* and *keep it concrete*. At Key Stage 2, mathematical problems and explanations often become more verbal and abstract and you will need to help the child use their visual strengths to compensate for any weaknesses in verbal comprehension.

For children with both language and literacy difficulties, it can

help to repeat and consolidate one form of number and algebra (such as adding or subtracting tens and units) rather than to jump around between different forms of calculation (as many mathematics schemes tend to do). Use *structured, multi-sensory cumulative teaching* to help it all make sense. Use *non-verbal modelling* to demonstrate setting out, using large squares and working from large scale to small as the child becomes more confident in handling written calculations. For children with severe writing difficulties, consider using sticky number labels, number lines, number squares and *highlighting* as *alternative means of recording*. *Teach reversals* if a child towards the end of Key Stage 1 is really struggling to remember which way round numerals should go.

AGE RANGE
Five to seven.

GROUP SIZE
Ten to 15 children.

LEARNING OBJECTIVE FOR ALL THE CHILDREN
● To write numerals from 0 to 9 correctly, tracing from top to bottom.

INDIVIDUAL LEARNING TARGET
● To identify the correct rotation of numerals up to 9.

Numeral detectives

Many children struggle to remember which way round numerals should go and this difficulty often persists for longer for children with dyslexia.

What you need
Two sets of large number cards 0 to 9, one correctly written and one with mistakes (see below); songs and rhymes with numbers up to ten.

Preparation
Select some number songs. Prepare one set of number cards full of mistakes – numbers written in reverse, upside down and so on.

What to do
Begin with songs which use numbers up to ten, such as 'One, Two, Three, Four, Five, Once I Caught a Fish Alive' or 'Ten Green Bottles'. As the children sing, hold up a numeral, sometimes making deliberate mistakes by using a number card with the wrong numeral on or which is the wrong way round. Explain that you cannot see what you are doing. Ask them to tell you if you are making a 'mistake'.

Now scatter the two sets of number cards 0 to 9 on the floor. Ask the children to help you out by taking turns to hold up a numeral from the floor when the rest of you sing it. Children watching can help by noticing if a 'mistake' card is chosen. Play the game plenty

of times, so that everyone has a chance to use the numerals and identify and correct errors. This will allow children with difficulties to grow in confidence. Play 'Numeral detectives'. Ask the children to close their eyes while you write a line of numerals on the whiteboard. Reverse the rotation of some of the numerals. When they open their eyes, ask them if they can spot your mistakes.

Demonstrate tracing numbers in the air from top to bottom, and encourage the children to mimic you. Can the other children recognise the number being traced?

Special support
Use repetition and multi-sensory approaches to teach the correct numeral shape by using finger painting or writing in sand.

Extension
Make 'Pelmanism', 'Snap' and 'Pairs' cards made out of different reversals and orientations of the same shape, letter or numeral – can the children match them *exactly*?

AGE RANGE
Five to seven.

GROUP SIZE
Whole group.

LEARNING OBJECTIVE FOR ALL THE CHILDREN
● To use and begin to read the vocabulary of comparing and ordering numbers.

INDIVIDUAL LEARNING TARGET
● To understand and respond to words, such as 'more than', 'same as', 'less than', 'greater', 'smaller' and so on.

How many...?

Children with language difficulties may need extra teaching of the vocabulary of mathematics. Try linking an abstract word to actions.

What you need
A large number of Multilink cubes; squared paper for a graph to be made by each child.

Preparation
Decide on the mathematical vocabulary that you want to teach.

What to do
Give the children and yourself varied numbers of bricks or Multilink cubes (four to 20). Count your cubes aloud and write up your total. Invite the children to do the same with their cubes. (Working in pairs will help less confident children.) Encourage the children to write down their totals. Ask the children questions, comparing your total with theirs. For example: Does anyone have the same number as you? Who has fewer cubes? Who has more than you?

Emphasise and repeat the mathematical vocabulary that you want the children to learn. Compile and display a list of this vocabulary.

Ask the children, with partners, to think of two questions to ask each other. The questions must be about their cubes and must use some of the listed vocabulary. Let the children ask and answer each other's questions. Ask the pairs to snowball into larger groups of four. One pair should now question the other pair. What do they learn? Do the partners have something to report – using mathematical vocabulary – to the rest of the class? Take feedback from the children, encouraging them to speak.

Invite each group of four to arrange their cubes on a table in order of size from least to most. The children can then stand behind their cubes to form a 'living graph'. Let each group explain its living graph to the rest of the class ('Jamie comes *first* – he has *six* – then Sam has *seven* so he's *second...*').

Ask the children to record their group results in individual graphs on squared paper (partner work may be more appropriate for some children). Encourage the children to write three sentences about their graphs, using some of the mathematical vocabulary from the chart. Consider providing questions for the children to answer.

Special support
Children with language difficulties may need prompting. Check understanding of vocabulary regularly, *tune into language levels* and provide practical demonstrations of difficult words where necessary.

Extension
Find out about other ways of recording results – for example: pie charts, bar charts and histograms.

AGE RANGE
Seven to nine.

GROUP SIZE
Any.

LEARNING OBJECTIVE FOR ALL THE CHILDREN
● To develop pencil and paper methods for additions that cannot, at this stage, be done mentally.

INDIVIDUAL LEARNING TARGET
● To calculate a simple tens and units sum correctly.

Add it up!

Children with dyslexia often become confused when having to remember how to set out numbers for calculations. Activities like this will help.

What you need

Prepared calculations involving the addition of two-digit numbers; familiarity with pencil and paper methods of addition (NNS supplement of examples).

What to do

Warm-up with mental addition of a single digit to a set of tens: for example, 20 + 6. Stress to the children how easy it is to add single digits to tens. Move to a calculation which involves crossing the tens boundary, for example, 28 + 7. Ask the children to explain to partners how they reach their answers. Show on the board your three mental stages:

Stage 1 – reach the next ten: 28 + <u>2</u> + 5 =
Stage 2 – cross the tens boundary: <u>30</u> + 5 =
Stage 3 – add a single digit to a set of tens: 3<u>5</u>.

Work through a few other examples together, before moving to two two-digit numbers, for example, 27 + 21.

Stage 1 – make tens: 27 + <u>20</u> + 1 =
Stage 2 – add to tens: <u>47</u> + 1=
Stage 3 – add a single digit: 48.

Work together on other examples. Introduce a calculation bringing further problems: 37 + 86. Can the children estimate the total? Will the calculation cross a new boundary? Show your mental process:

Stage 1 – make a set of tens: 37 + <u>80</u> + 6 =
Stage 2 – cross the hundreds boundary: <u>117</u> + 6 =
Stage 3 – cross a tens boundary: <u>120</u> + 3 =
Stage 4 – add a single digit: 123.

Discuss how these numbers are becoming difficult to remember. Demonstrate linear recording, using arrows and jumps between numbers. Suggest that column recording would be more efficient and demonstrate it (NNS supplement of examples). Explain the content of each line, and give the children useful memory tips:

● put everyone in the proper team (units under units and so on).
● look for tens
● grab a hundred when you can
● little numbers are easy to add on later.

Special support

Provide visual prompt cards for children who have weak working memories and always work a few examples with them before setting written exercises.

Extension

Extend to written calculations using three or four columns.

AGE RANGE
Seven to nine.

GROUP SIZE
Whole group.

LEARNING OBJECTIVE FOR ALL THE CHILDREN
● To identify two simple fractions with a total of 1.

INDIVIDUAL LEARNING TARGET
● To understand and respond to words, such as 'half', 'quarter', 'fifth', 'percentage', 'multiple' and 'factor'.

Snakes and adders

Children with language difficulties may need extra teaching and practice when it comes to managing language of a new topic, such as fractions.

What you need
Prepared fraction lines; playing-card-sized pieces of card (about 24 for each pair of children).

Preparation
Make three fraction lines for display, each line consisting of fractions totalling 1. The first line should be divided into halves and quarters; the second into thirds and sixths, and the third into fifths and tenths.

What to do
Display the fraction line divided into halves and quarters. Ask the children appropriate questions, for example, 'If you have one quarter how many more quarters do you need to make one whole?'

Record answers in fraction notation (for example, $\frac{1}{4} + \frac{3}{4} = 1$). Display the other two fraction lines, doing similar oral work and ensuring that everyone is using appropriate vocabulary. Leave the fraction lines on display. Now ask the children, working with partners, to write down, in fraction notation, ten to 15 different ways to make one whole from the fraction lines, for example, $\frac{2}{5} + \frac{3}{5} = 1$.

Check that the children's fractions are correct, before letting them move on to making a game with their ways of totalling 1. Give out the pieces of card to each pair of children. Tell them they are going to make their pairs of fractions into pairs of playing cards. On one side of a card they should write part of their fraction sentence and, on the other side, a colourful snake. That fraction card can only total 1 if it can find its partner. So on another card the children write the other fraction needed and, on its reverse side, another snake (let's call it an adder!) the same colour.

Continue until each couple have made ten to 15 different pairs of cards, each pair representing different ways of making 1 from two fractions.

Ask the children to spread their cards out, fraction-side up. Can they see two fractions that equal 1? Turn the cards over to check – if they are right they will find a snake and an adder that match!

Special support
Saying the answers as a small group, chanting as a class and sharing answers with a partner can all be helpful to children who find it difficult to give answers on their own.

Extension
Try challenging the children to use three cards to equal 1, for example $\frac{2}{7} + \frac{1}{7} + \frac{4}{7} = 1$.

AGE RANGE
Nine to eleven.

GROUP SIZE
Whole group.

LEARNING OBJECTIVE FOR ALL THE CHILDREN
● To read and know what each digit in a number represents, and partition numbers into thousands, hundreds, tens and ones.

INDIVIDUAL LEARNING TARGET
● To understand which of two digits is in the tens place and which is in the units place.

Know your place

Place value can be very muddling for children who find it hard to sort out left and right directions. The trick is to provide verbal rules for children to talk themselves through what they are doing.

What you need
Single-digit cards and place-value cards – 'th', 'h', 't', 'u' (one per child); a washing line to hang across classroom; three- and four-digit numbers to peg on line; large place-value signs – 'th', 'h', 't', 'u'.

Preparation
Decide where to position the large place-value signs.

What to do
Make the session fast-moving so that the children experience varied numbers. Begin with easy three-digit numbers. Peg numbers on a line and identify the hundreds, tens and units numbers.

Ask the children to put themselves into threes and play 'Where do I stand?' Give each group a three-digit number. Each child in the group should hold up a number card for one of the three digits. Hang three signs ('hundreds', 'tens', 'units') side by side at the front of the class, so that children can stand beneath them. Does each digit stand under the correct sign? Find useful memory tips:
● the richest digit leads the line (hundreds)
● you are stuck in the middle because there is someone richer and poorer (tens)
● The poorest comes last (units).

Move to four-digit numbers. Play the game again with groups of four. Offer to buy digits. Do the children know their value? Are they worth £40 or £400? Use memory tips, for example, 'I am worth ten times more than the one below me in line'.

Give each group of four children four cards, each bearing a single digit between 0 and 9, and four-place value cards. Each card must have on it <u>one</u> of these: 'thousands' (th); 'hundreds' (h); 'tens' (t); 'units' (u). After the groups have shared out cards and digits, ask them to make a number. Then let the groups take turns displaying their number to the class, standing in the correct place for the digit card and place-value card held.

Special support
Less confident children may prefer to display their numbers to you or your classroom helper.

Extension
Let the groups experiment, exchanging digits or place value. What new numbers can they make?

AGE RANGE
Nine to eleven.

GROUP SIZE
Whole group.

LEARNING OBJECTIVE FOR ALL THE CHILDREN
● To recognise the equivalence between the decimal and fraction forms.

INDIVIDUAL LEARNING TARGET
● To match simple equivalences such half and 0.5.

Equivalent fun

This activity helps children understand and use equivalences between fractions, decimals and percentages in a concrete way.

What you need
A washing line to hang across the classroom; fraction cards to peg on the line; a calculator (one per child or per pair of children); a prepared list of about ten fractions to use for the card game; pieces of white card – double the size of a playing card (about ten pieces for each pair of children); scissors.

Preparation
String a line across the classroom.

What to do
Revise the terms decimal and fraction. Use a washing line and peg out some fractions. Ask the children to help identify them. Leave the cards on the line to help the children as you ask them to use their individual whiteboards to convert your words into fraction notation. Dictate a list of ten or so simple fractions. Give plenty of 'show me' practice to build the confidence of children with difficulties. Then let the children work in pairs, testing each other. How many fractions can they say and write accurately after five minutes?

Move to decimals. Write on the board a decimal – for example, 0.35. Do the children understand it? Demonstrate representing it in fraction form. Work on other examples, perhaps helping the children with oral answers by using a multiple-choice format for example, 'Is 0.3 equivalent to thirty tenths, <u>three tenths</u> or three thousandths? Demonstrate how the decimal equivalent can be found by entering the fraction into a calculator and interpreting the decimal display. Model this use of a calculator.

Give each pair of children about ten cards. Ask them to use only one side of the cards. They should write a fraction in the top half and its decimal equivalent in the bottom half. Write a list of fractions for the children to copy. Suggest that the children try predicting the decimal equivalents before confirming results with calculators.

Once one side of every card is complete, the cards should be cut in half – so that each card bears only one form of notation. Explain that you want the children to devise a card game which will give them practice in using equivalent fractions and decimal forms.

Special support
Use a visual reminder of common equivalences on a wall chart using *clever colours* to aid the memory of children with difficulties.

Extension
Plan a further session for making the games.

HISTORY

The strand of history has been included because of the problems that children with both literacy and language difficulties might experience. While children with dyslexia might excel when you encourage oral responses, they might have more difficulties in handling written source material and in recording their work. History topic work lends itself beautifully to mind maps and alternative means of recording, such as tape recording, role-play and the use of visual displays and oral presentations. It can be used to build self-esteem by setting up peer support and small-team work, and encouraging certain children to scribe and to read and others to contribute orally and practically.

Take care when planning source materials to individualise texts whenever you can, making use of clever colours and highlighting salient information. Revising and recapping on work covered will give you the opportunity to teach study skills in a multi-sensory way. Enlarge dense written text where possible using a photocopier and make use of multi-sensory source material as well as paper sources, perhaps using ICT or real artefacts, photographs, and video clips.

Children who have difficulties with language sometimes take a while to master the use of verb tenses for the past, the future, passive and active. For this reason, you need to be aware that

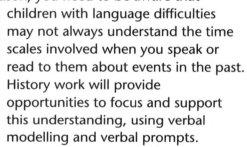

children with language difficulties may not always understand the time scales involved when you speak or read to them about events in the past. History work will provide opportunities to focus and support this understanding, using verbal modelling and verbal prompts.

You can adapt visual timetables to become a way of recording historical events, making simple comic strips of key historical features.

Make use of historical role-play to extend imagination and to facilitate joining in. Drama and role-play are excellent ways of encouraging children with poor language skills and inflexible ways of thinking to tune into what it is like to be someone else and allow you to teach social skills. They also help you to keep it concrete and to help the child link words to actions in order to gain a fuller understanding.

You might find it helpful for the children to work in pairs so that they can support each other's weaknesses and share their strengths. Friends can scribe for each other and pool their good ideas. in a similar way, set up small groups to be 'research teams'.

AGE RANGE
Five to seven.

GROUP SIZE
Whole group.

LEARNING OBJECTIVE FOR ALL THE CHILDREN
● To think about the past, using common words and phrases relating to the passing of time.

INDIVIDUAL LEARNING TARGET
● To use the past tense correctly when talking about past experiences.

In my past

Children with language difficulties may find verb tenses hard to understand. This simple activity about life stories can help them sort these out.

What you need
Children's artefacts from home; artefacts from you and your teaching assistant.

Preparation
Ask the children to do a preliminary homework task, involving them and their parents or carers: they need to find out about a toy from their past. Most of them will still have an old teddy, soft book, toy car or doll, which they used to play with as a toddler or baby. They will need to think, or to ask adults, about how they used the toy, when it was given to them, or why they liked it. Ask the children to bring these memories, and the toy, to school.

What to do
Explain that you are all going to tell one another about your toys from the past. Use your own experiences and your classroom assistant's experiences as models. Stress how you are talking about using your toys in the past. Pick out and make a chart of some of the words and phrases that you use. Emphasise past tenses of verbs.

Ask the children to tell you about how they played with their toys. Have a helpful list of speaking prompts on display, which will guide children towards using verbs in the past tense.

Try these:
● When I was little, I…
● I liked to…
● I kept…
● I used to…
● Before I could talk, I…

Encourage the children to use their toys as visual aids. Some children may find the task easier if prompted by well-worded questions which guide them towards an answer in the past tense.

Ask the children to do a piece of writing and drawing of their toys. Use a writing frame such as the example above. Extend the presentations to a living display, in which the toys and short pieces of writing are on show, with the toys' owners on hand to answer questions.

Special support
If a child answers in the incorrect tense, model the correct way of saying it and encourage them as they repeat it.

Extension
Discuss with the children how you can find out about toys from even longer ago. Are there grandparents or friends of the school willing to visit and tell you about toys from their past?

AGE RANGE
Five to seven.

GROUP SIZE
Whole group.

LEARNING OBJECTIVE FOR ALL THE CHILDREN
● To learn about the main events and results of the Great Fire of London.

INDIVIDUAL LEARNING TARGET
● To join in a simple role-play and speak in the role of someone else.

Travel back in time

Role-play can be a powerful way to encourage children to think about history in action and develop their imagination, especially those who find language and flexible thought difficult.

What you need
Background information on the Great Fire of London.

Preparation
Talk about the Great Fire of London: how it broke out in 1666; how it spread quickly because of wooden buildings packed closely together; how the wind spread the fire; how some people took shelter in buildings made of stone (such as churches); how people escaped by getting to the river; how the fire went out finally because the wind stopped; how the city of London had to be rebuilt; how it was designed by Christopher Wren. Explain that we know so much about the fire because of Samuel Pepys who saw the fire and wrote about it in his diary.

What to do
Explain to the children that you want them to 'become' the people living in London at the time of the Great Fire. Talk about some of the people involved:
● a child, living in one of the squashed-together wooden houses
● King Charles II, safe, but seeing his most important city being destroyed by flames
● a person running away from the fire towards the river
● a person begging for a place on a boat
● a man trying to save his family
● Samuel Pepys, a rich man, who moves his family away to safety by boat and then travels back along the river to see the fire for himself. At night he writes his diary
● Samuel Pepys's wife
● a person loading his possessions on to a boat on the river
● Christopher Wren, a clever architect and friend of King Charles II, planning how to rebuild the city.

Ask the children to work with a partner. Each must choose a character to be; then the two people must talk to each other. (Charles II talks to Wren about rebuilding the city. Pepys tells his wife what he has seen today.) Let the class eavesdrop on some conversations. Do the children understand how people felt in 1666?

Special support
Choose alternative means of recording a diary for children with dyslexia so that they can still excel.

Extension
Ask the children to write a diary in the voice of their character.

AGE RANGE
Seven to nine.

GROUP SIZE
Whole group.

LEARNING OBJECTIVE FOR ALL THE CHILDREN
● To develop understanding of historical events.

INDIVIDUAL LEARNING TARGET
● To create a simple mind map based on a historical topic.

Read all about it!

Mind maps are an excellent way of appealing to all learning styles – looking, listening and doing. They also support pupils with dyslexia.

What you need
An OHP slide of photocopiable page 46; individual copies of photocopiable page 87.

Preparation
Use this activity as an introduction to Roman invaders and settlers.

What to do
Remind the children of how mind maps work – photocopiable page 46 is an example. Highlight important points: the main subject is in the centre, the long branches name connected subjects and the shorter branches add detail. Demonstrate how every word can be traced back to the main subject.

Work together on a new mind map. Choose a famous historical figure, for example, Henry VIII. Put Henry's name at the centre. Draw four main branches and label them: 'Marriages', 'Children', 'Religion' and 'Palaces'. Share ideas for the short branches ('six', 'beheadings', 'divorces'; 'Mary', 'Elizabeth', 'Edward'; 'Catholic', 'England', 'Pope'; 'London', 'Greenwich', 'Thames'). Show how these short branches could have shorter twigs coming off them as smaller details are added.

Explain that you are beginning history work on invaders and settlers, starting with the Romans. Now put the children into groups of about four. Challenge them to see what they can discover about the Romans in Britain from a newspaper. Give each child a copy of the photocopiable page. Suggest reading it with a partner (this will help less confident readers) before discussing it in a group of four.

Explain that you want each group to produce its own mind map. Suggest rough planning first. The final version, on a large piece of paper, should make use of colours to identify one long branch of the tree from another; all the shorter branches coming from that long branch should be in the same colour. Remind the children that, as branches become smaller, so should the print reduce in size. Let each group present and talk the class through their mind map.

Special support
Encourage oral responses for children with a literacy difficulty in order to build self-esteem. They can be valuable team members in practical aspects of the mind-map task, such as checking that the right colour and branching is used.

Extension
Set a new topic and ask the children to research it on the internet using a mind map to summarise their findings.

AGE RANGE
Seven to nine.

GROUP SIZE
Whole group.

LEARNING OBJECTIVE FOR ALL THE CHILDREN
● To find about the past from a range of sources of information.

INDIVIDUAL LEARNING TARGET
● To visit websites for specific information and to produce a simple written summary.

A voice from the past

Children with dyslexia benefit from the using of ICT which can be used to assist research and recording.

What you need
Computers with internet access – enough for the children to work in small groups.

Preparation
Explore internet websites on your chosen history unit. A helpful site would be www.museumoflondon.org.uk. To access the site, click on 'Learning' and then select: 'Digging up the Romans'.

What to do
Tell the children the objective: to find out more about people in the past. Check whether the children are confident in their use of the internet. Demonstrate ICT skills, such as scrolling, using hyperlinks and moving between windows.

This activity focuses on the Romans but could easily be adapted to the Tudors or another period. Remind the children of their mind maps (see page 83). Point out that mind maps are good starting points, providing headline information. Explain that they are going to discover more about the Romans by investigating archaeological evidence which will reveal facts about life in Roman London.
Say that you are going to publish a newspaper from Londinium and that you want the children to be Roman voices from the past. Information in the newspaper articles must be authentic. Draw a mind map with seven long branches, labelling them as follows: 'People', 'Town life', 'Invasion and settlement', 'Army', 'Beliefs', 'Crafts', 'Roads and trade'.

Divide the children into small groups of three or four and let them choose a theme. Provide working tips: taking turns using the computer mouse; making brief notes; making sketches and diagrams; reading parts of the screen aloud to one another (a help to children with reading problems). In later sessions they will need to put their material together and to agree on group roles. Plan a newspaper layout so that groups can enter their articles.

Special support
Group collaboration means that that not everyone has to be a proficient reader or writer: a sketch may be a reminder of a fact, to be contributed orally, while another person writes it down.

Extension
Find out more about journalism. Meet your deadline and publish!

AGE RANGE
Nine to eleven.

GROUP SIZE
Whole group.

LEARNING OBJECTIVE FOR ALL THE CHILDREN
● To understand why Drake chose to circumnavigate the world.

INDIVIDUAL LEARNING TARGET
● To make meaningful and grammatical additions to a partial text.

Close the gap

Children with both literacy and language difficulties benefit from cloze procedure to help them focus on meaning and context of written work.

What you need
Individual copies of the log (with missing words) from Drake's ship.

Preparation
Write a text to present to the class as an original source such as:

---

15 January 1580
There is much concern about the (1) w _ _ _ _ er: a storm is blowing hard and even more (2) r _ _ _ looks likely. We are close to the land of King (3) _ _ _ _ ip of Spain, so rich   (4) _ _ _ _ _ sh ships are being watched for. Now is the time to use our best (5) _ _ _ esc _ _ _ _ . There may be valuable (6) tr _ _ _ _ _ _ to take.
Our brave (7) _ _ _ _ ain is determined that he will be the (8) _ _ _ _ _ seaman to travel around the whole (9) _ _ _ _ _ . If he is (10) _ _ _ _ essf _ _ , it (11) w _ _ _ bring great pleasure to (12) El _ _ _ _ _ _ _ _ , our (13) _ _ _ _ _ and (14) Dr _ _ _ will be (15) rew _ _ _ ed with (16) g _ _ _ t sums of (17) _ _ _ _ y.

As the log would have been written in Tudor times, typing the document in an appropriate font should make it look more authentic.

What to do
Tell the children the Museum of History has discovered what could be an important source of information – an extract from an officer's log. Research has revealed the writer to be a naval officer on Drake's ship – an amazing discovery! However, the document has been damaged, by time and seawater, so there are missing words. For this to be a valuable historical source, those words are needed. Can the children?

Let the children work with partners. They need to write out a completed source for the museum. Remind them that books and history work on Drake may help but they must think about what would make sense in the gaps. Will the museum be pleased with the results? Finally, reveal the solutions to the missing words.

Special support
Make use of peer support, partners reading aloud to each other may help children with difficulties.

Extension
Consider having a harder text ready for children who finish quickly.

AGE RANGE
Nine to eleven.

GROUP SIZE
Whole group.

LEARNING OBJECTIVE FOR ALL THE CHILDREN
● To appreciate the dangers and discomforts of life at sea.

INDIVIDUAL LEARNING TARGET
● To translate a paragraph of text from code.

Break the code

Children with scanning difficulties benefit from practice in tracking and remembering visually presented information. This simple code activity provides that opportunity.

What you need
A diary text (example supplied) which you have converted into code.

Preparation
Write a text describing the experience of one of the ordinary members of Drake's crew. Make sure that the text describes some important aspects of life at sea: food, punishments, superstitions and disease. The following would be a good example.

There is much fear now among us men, for our two black cats have died. With them gone, bad luck is sure to befall us, and an enemy or a sea monster will get us.
With no cat to kill them, the rats are everywhere, crawling over us at night, but rum kills my dread of them.
My mouth is cracked and covered with sores and there is pain from a carbuncle. I feel weak as I climb to the Crows-nest, but my job is look-out and I am afraid to be caught slacking at my work lest the Captain order that I be lashed. Last week a man died under the whip.

Now put the text into a code. Make the code fairly straightforward, perhaps A=1, B=2 and so on.

What to do
Explain that ordinary seamen may also have kept diaries. If they had complaints about their conditions, they would have been wise to keep them to themselves because discipline was harsh.

Present the children with this situation: an officer on board Drake's ship has found part of a young sailor's diary and wants to know what he has written. He knows that the sailor can read, write and count. Can the children help the officer to crack the code and decipher the message? You may decide to provide the children with a key for some of the numbers: 1=A; 7=G; 22=V.

Suggest that the children work with partners: code-breakers rarely work alone! What do the children find out about life for the ordinary sailor on Drake's long voyage?

Special support
Break steps down by providing a visual copy of the code for a child with difficulties to apply word by word or sentence by sentence.

Extension
Can they write their own coded account of of life at sea?

THE ROMAN

Can the weather get worse?

Soldiers are suffering in the fearsome conditions of this country. It is impossible to keep warm in the terrible conditions we are enduring. There is a dread that, even when summer arrives here, the sun will lack the heat of our own Mediterranean climate.

Worse may be in store, for there is talk of soldiers being posted further north. Rumours speak of a wall being built to protect the land we have captured from the Picts, the fiercest enemy we face here. The wall is likely to stretch across the coldest regions of England, and will be constructed and guarded by our brave soldiers.

It is known that the northern territory is even colder than here in Eboracum. How will our soldiers survive in their tunics and sandals?

THINKING OF FOOD

Fortunate families are now having the taste of home shipped from across the sea, but poorer families must rely on the local produce.

Certainly, local fruits lack the taste of our homeland's succulent grapes, peaches and melons. However, think imaginatively and even in this land you will be able to eat healthily.

Cooking tips:

Keep your diet simple – you will stay healthier.

Rely mainly on vegetables – turnips, onions, potatoes, beans and mushrooms all produce hearty, warming soups.

Use wheat to make filling portions of porridge and bread.

Try pork. It is a meat that is available cheaply and, once cooked slowly in the ashes of your brick oven, will be nourishing and tasty.

GEOGRAPHY

Geography has been included because of the problems that children with dyslexia might have when handling the literacy element of this strand. It also presents opportunities for you to encourage oral responses and develop alternative means of recording. Geography topic work lends itself beautifully to mind maps, role-play, the use of visual displays, oral presentations, audio and video diaries and the use of fantasy. Geography can be presented in a motivating and multi-sensory way in order to build self-esteem. You can encourage children to work with partners and make use of peer support. By organising small 'research teams' or 'think tanks' you can help children develop multiple roles when finding out and presenting, encouraging certain children to scribe and to read and others to contribute orally and practically.

Once again, you will need to individualise texts whenever you can, making use of clever colours and highlighting salient information. Enlarge dense written text where possible, make use of multi-sensory source material and use ICT. Photographs, film and video clips can bring environments to life in a meaningful way for everyone and ensure that you are appealing to each learning style – seeing, listening and doing.

Children who have difficulties with language sometimes take a while to master the use of abstract positional (for example, 'beyond', 'within') and directional (for example, 'east', 'west') language and there are plenty of opportunities within geography to practise and support this using verbal modelling, verbal prompts and keeping it concrete. Make use of role-play and fantasy to extend imagination and to facilitate joining in. Whole geography topics can be covered almost effortlessly by having the class monkey mascot on safari or travelling with a migratory herd of wildebeest, with all the messages and reports that flow back and forth! The Power of Fantasy in Early Learning by Jenny Tyrell (see pages 95 to 96) is useful here.

At Key Stage 2, much geography topic work involves the children suggesting appropriate geographical questions or issues and then making suggestions for possible ways of finding out and investigating. Use this as an opportunity for showing all the children how to design mind maps and make it a priority to teach study skills. Though this will benefit all the children, it will be especially helpful for children who have dyslexia or who have had language difficulties when they were younger.

AGE RANGE
Five to seven.

GROUP SIZE
Whole group.

LEARNING
OBJECTIVE FOR ALL
THE CHILDREN
● To express views
about making the
area safer.
● To recognise ways
of changing the
environment.

INDIVIDUAL
LEARNING TARGET
● To use and
understand words,
such as 'behind', 'on
top of', 'underneath'.

Watch out!

Children with language difficulties may need to be taught simple directional words, such as 'in', 'on, 'under' and 'behind'. This simple activity based on the classroom layout will help them.

What you need
Identified dangers for children in the school grounds (perhaps placed deliberately); proposals for improving safety.

Preparation
Take the children on a tour of the school grounds. Explain that you are thinking about safety. Identify possible hazards, but keep the tone low-key. Your blacklist could include:
● a cycle path that people might walk across
● tree stumps to trip over
● a hard netball under the post (ready to roll in front of someone)
● slippery playgrounds for falling on
● rubbish next to the bin instead of in it (it could be slipped on)
● paper underneath the bench for someone to slip on
● a hard football between goalposts (is it safe for a young child?)
● a heavy box on top of the window ledge (will it fall down?)
● a skipping rope across a gap between two benches
● a car park next to the playground.

What to do
Back in the classroom, work together listing unsafe areas or items you have spotted. List key direction words. Explain to the children that the headteacher wants the school environment to be safe. Therefore, the headteacher needs to know about potential problems and useful solutions. Thought-storm a few solutions:
● white painted lines marking special areas for playing ball
● polite, reminder notices
● clearing of items
● special tracks for playtime runners and walkers.
Discuss methods of presentation – perhaps before and after posters, in which the danger is identified, and then the solution. Let the children use talk partners to discuss one or two of the problems. Ask partners to plan what will be on their poster and what their sentences will say. Emphasise the use of key direction words. Ask them to present their plans orally to the class.

Special support
Be discreet: children with language difficulties may be happier making oral presentations to only you. Keep it concrete by using a demonstration to show what positional words mean.

Extension
When the children have produced the posters, they must plan how to persuade the headteacher of the need to implement the changes!

AGE RANGE
Five to seven.

GROUP SIZE
Whole group.

LEARNING OBJECTIVE FOR ALL THE CHILDREN
● To describe the features of the local environment.
● To express views on the features.

INDIVIDUAL LEARNING TARGET
● To enjoy early writing for a purpose.

Inspectors on the loose!

Children who struggle with writing need it to be extra fun and to have a personal meaning. Finding out about your neighbourhood can inspire this.

What you need

A large-scale map of area around your school; adult helpers for a field visit to the area; computers (one for each pair of children); camera (digital, if possible).

Preparation

Talk to the children about the local neighbourhood. Can they think of any important features? Do they know of any recent changes? Is it a good environment?

What to do

Explain that the children are to become environmental inspectors. In pairs they will be writing one page of a report on the local environment. The inspectors have to investigate the local area. Agree what the inspectors will be doing:

● looking at what the area is like
● noticing the types of buildings
● identifying important features
● spotting changes that are occurring
● making a note of places which they find particularly attractive or unattractive (and recording their reasons)
● deciding if this is a good environment.

Use a large-scale map to show the children the route/s that they will be following. Make the trip and record their thoughts in words, numbers, diagrams and sketches. Use the school digital camera to photograph places that the children identify as attractive or unattractive.

Back in the classroom, give the children time to talk to their partners about their notes. Then ask them to write up their findings. Providing a writing frame with a multiple-choice element would be useful, such as:

This area is a _____ (good/bad/quite good) place to live and work. Most of the buildings are _____ (old/new).

Let the children type out their reports. If your camera is digital, pre-load a chosen photograph on to each pair's computer. Otherwise develop the photographs for the children to include in their reports.

Special support

Writing frames and offering multiple choices are helpful approaches as they inspire confidence.

Extension

Give some of the children the task of putting together the whole report.

AGE RANGE
Seven to nine.

GROUP SIZE
Whole group.

LEARNING OBJECTIVE FOR ALL THE CHILDREN
● To use and interpret maps.

INDIVIDUAL LEARNING TARGET
● To learn simple brain-gym exercises (see reference on pages 96).

Left or right?

Children with dyslexia benefit from work on rights and lefts – a simple map activity can make this fun and provide an opportunity to build in some brain-gym warming-up exercises as well.

What you need
Large-scale maps of your local area, showing the school site; aerial photographs of the area; copies of the area maps (enough for one for each group of three children); large space (such as the hall).

Preparation
Begin with some brain-gym exercises to prepare the children's bodies and brains for learning. Keep the movements quick and fun:
Cross crawl: lift one knee and touch it with the opposite hand, crossing the body's midline with that hand. Repeat this with the other knee and hand.
Lazy 8: imagine an '8' shape on its side. Stretch out one arm in front of you and raise your thumb, level with your nose. Go up to the left and trace the shape of the lying down, lazy 8, keeping your head still and following your thumb with your eyes. Use one hand, then the other, and finally both together.
   (Brain-gym exercises taken from 'Exercise Your Mind' by Alan Heath from an article in Junior Education, November 2004.)

What to do
Show the children a large-scale map of the local area. Identify and mark important points: the church, community centre and so on.

Use the aerial photographs and discuss how the sites can be identified (from their shape). Ask the children to locate the school. Explain that you want them to work out some school walks. The school site must always be the start and finish point and the walks should include places that are easy to identify. Revise terminology, in particular 'right' and 'left'.
Give each group of three children a map. Ask them to keep notes on the route they are working out, and stress the value of diagrams and pictorial representation. Emphasise the importance of accurate directions. Encourage them to 'walk' the pretend journey themselves in the school hall, rehearsing points along the route and checking direction.

Special support
Make use of mnemonics by inventing useful memory tips for children with difficulties to remember left and right.

Extension
Work with the children to produce a class book of 'School Walks'.

AGE RANGE
Seven to nine.

GROUP SIZE
Whole group.

LEARNING OBJECTIVE FOR ALL THE CHILDREN
● To learn about weather conditions around the world.

INDIVIDUAL LEARNING TARGET
● To be motivated to engage in reading and writing for a purpose.

Monkey's travels

The use of fantasy allows you to travel anywhere you wish in your teaching and learning! Here is an activity based on letters to and from Monkey who is travelling abroad.

What you need

A large map of the world; a globe; individual copies of a newspaper's weather round-up from around the world; individual copies of a map of Europe; a large supply of blank postcards.

Preparation

Investigate places on a world map and globe. Identify some places which are popular tourist destinations, such as Paris, Madrid, Oslo, Brussels or Majorca. Ask the children if they know which countries and continent the places are in? Discuss holiday visits to these places by yourself or the children. What do the children know about the weather in these places? Do the children know where reliable weather readings can be found? (The internet or a newspaper.) Use a newspaper to find out about the weather in places on the previous day (The Times has a helpful weather section). Discuss differences from the temperatures in your area.

What to do

Set a scenario: Monkey has decided to make a grand tour of Europe so he has gone on holiday. He is sending back postcards to his pal,

Koala, telling her about the weather and saying where he plans to go next. Koala has a newspaper so she can offer advice about the weather and what clothes he'll need but her information is correct.

Explain to the children that you want them – working in pairs – to write the postcards between Monkey and Koala. Give them time to work out a holiday itinerary for Monkey, with a route that brings him back to his starting point. Share results, making sure that itineraries are manageable in length.

Then Monkey and Koala should complete their postcards. The partners may enjoy working together on what each postcard will say but encourage each character to do their own writing. Emphasise that Koala's weather reports need to be accurate so they must be based on figures from the newspaper. Let the class listen to some of the completed messages.

Special support

Use peer support: one partner to scribe and the other to dictate. Provide lists of keywords for weak spellers.

Extension

Find out about simple methods for predicting the weather (such as barometers, fir cones, seaweed).

AGE RANGE
Nine to eleven.

GROUP SIZE
Whole group.

LEARNING OBJECTIVE FOR ALL THE CHILDREN
● To draw up reasoned plans to present solutions, proposing environmental change in an area.

INDIVIDUAL LEARNING TARGET
● To present information in different ways.

Tackling traffic

Children with dyslexia can excel in topic work that involves different ways of presenting and recording. Here are some ideas.

What you need
Information about a local high-street area and its traffic issues.

Preparation
Focus on a local area familiar to the children. Select a street which is busy and presents a range of traffic issues because of the wide range of its use, with shops, cars, pedestrians, public and private buildings. Discuss with the children the traffic problems and try to make a visit to the street so that they can collect and record evidence.

What to do
Explain that the town council is concerned about local traffic issues. In particular, many people would like the main street (that they visited) to be closed to traffic. Do the children think this is a good idea? Discuss the advantages and disadvantages. Encourage them to recognise that different users have different needs. Identify user groups: drivers, pedestrians, shoppers, shopkeepers, residents and varied age groups. Discuss how these needs differ.

Explain that you want the children to form groups of four or five. They could belong to the same user group or be a mixture of people; they should try to think in their roles. You want them to work together to present a proposal to the town council in favour of or against road closure. It is important that a solution to the traffic problem is arrived at. Can they produce a workable plan? Thought-storm some ways to present a proposal:
● talking
● using visual aids
● using a model
● putting forward evidence
● graph of data
● computer-generated images.

Give the groups plenty of time to prepare their presentations, making sure that all members of a group are involved. Ask the children to plan how and when they will use each member of the group. Stress the importance of clarity.

Let the children make and listen to the presentations. Help the class to arrive at a reasoned conclusion.

Special support
Use partners instead of groups so that you can break steps down, provide reassurance and tune into language levels.

Extension
Help the children write a clearly reasoned report, using the computer to create a clear summary of their findings.

AGE RANGE
Nine to eleven.

GROUP SIZE
Whole group.

LEARNING OBJECTIVE FOR ALL THE CHILDREN
● To learn how the environment affects the nature of human activity.

INDIVIDUAL LEARNING TARGET
● To record an audio guide to describe natural conditions.

Talking guides

Children who are not fluent in reading and writing can participate fully and successfully in orally presented topics.

What you need
Tape recorders and blank tapes; background information on the Lake District (or other mountain environment).

Preparation
Carry out geography work on a mountain environment – such as the Lake District. Talk about what the place is like, its climate, population and their occupations. Point out the importance of tourism to an area such as the Lake District.

What to do
Explain to the children that you, as co-ordinator of tourism in the Lake District, are keen to produce guide material for young people planning a camping holiday in this mountain environment. You want the visitors to understand the importance of considering the nature of the environment they are visiting.

Discuss with the children the drawbacks of a guide book (it can lack appeal or practicality). Can the children think of a more exciting way to give guidance? Do visitors have to read the advice? Prompt the children to consider the use of audio material.
Thought-storm ideas for points that the audio guide could cover: weather, clothing, food, danger, safety precautions, accidents, suitable equipment, transport to area, local knowledge, adult help.

You could thought-storm ways to present information on the audio guide or you may prefer to let groups think of their own, original formats. Possible formats could include:
● a number of voices in a question-and-answer session
● role-play and drama
● interviews.

Divide the class into groups of four or five. The groups need to decide on three or four aspects of the camping holiday to deal with check any information they are unsure of decide on division of roles, and presentation, and work out the order and format of their guide. They should then rehearse. Agree on a time limit – perhaps about three to five minutes – for each audio guide. Let the groups make their recordings. Afterwards the class can listen to one another.

Special support
Move from group to group, ensuring that every group member is involved and to facilitate joining in. Support planning and persistence and offer reassurance to less confident learners.

Extension
Plan an imaginary mountain expedition.

RECOMMENDED RESOURCES

BOOKS FOR ADULTS

● Understanding Special Educational Needs: A Guide for Student Teachers by Michael Farrell (RoutledgeFalmer) – includes chapters on literacy difficulties and ICT.

● The Really Useful Literacy Book – Being Creative with Literacy in the Primary Classroom by Tony Martin, Chira Lovat and Glynis Purnell (RoutledgeFalmer).

● Speech and Language Difficulties by Hannah Mortimer from the series Special Needs in the Early Years (Scholastic).

● Day-to-Day Dyslexia in the Classroom (second edition) by Joy Pollock, Elisabeth Waller and Rody Politt (RoutledgeFalmer).

● Specific Learning Difficulties (Dyslexia): Challenges and Responses by Peter Pumfrey and Rea Reason (NFER-Nelson).

● Helping Children with Reading and Spelling: A Special Needs Manual by Rea Reason and Rene Boote (Routledge).

● Effective Teaching and Learning in the Classroom – A Practical Guide to Brain Compatible Learning by Sara Shaw and Trevor Hawes (Optimal Learning series). Available from Optimal Learning, PO Box 12, Leicester LE2 5AE. Email: THESERVICES@COMPUSERVE.COM (for helpful information on learning styles).

● Working with Children with Specific Learning Difficulties in the Early Years by Dorothy Smith (QEd) – also most valuable at KS1.

● Specific Learning Difficulties by Dorothy Smith (NASEN).

● The Power of Fantasy in Early Learning by Jenny Tyrell (RoutledgeFalmer) – motivational literacy in KS1.

● Commonsense Methods for Children with Special Educational Needs (fourth edition) by Peter Westwood (RoutledgeFalmer).

GOVERNMENT GUIDANCE

● DfEE and QCA: The National Curriculum: Handbook for primary teachers in England Key Stages 1 and 2.

● DfEE: The National Numeracy Strategy (ref NNFT).

● DfEE: Supporting the Target Setting Process (ref DfEE 0065/2001) – all about P scales.

● DfES: Special Educational Needs Code of Practice (ref DfES 581/2001).

● DfES: SEN Toolkit (ref 0558/2001).

● DfES: The National Literacy Strategy (ref 0500/2001) and Early Literacy Support Programme (ref 0650 2001).

● DfES: The National Literacy and Numeracy Strategies: Including All Children in the Literacy Hour and Daily Mathematics Lesson (ref 0465/2002).

● QCA: Planning, Teaching and Assessing the Curriculum for Pupils with Learning Difficulties (2001).

NATIONAL ORGANISATIONS

● Association for All Speech Impaired Children (AFASIC): 2nd floor, 50/52 Great Sutton Street, London EC1V ODJ. Website: **www.afasic.org.uk.**

● The British Dyslexia Association: 98 London Road, Reading RG1 5AU. Website: www.bda-dyslexia.org.uk.

● The Dyslexia Institute: Park House, Wick Road, Egham, Surrey TW20 OHN. Website: www.dyslexia-inst.org.uk.

● The Helen Arkell Dyslexia Centre: Frensham, Farnham, Surrey GU10 3BW. Website: www.arkellcentre.org.uk.

● The Royal College of Speech and Language Therapists: 2 White Hart Yard, London, SE1 1NX. Tel: 020 7378 1200

● The Department for Education and Skills (DfES) (for parent information and for Government circulars and advice). Website: www.dfes.gov.uk.

● Makaton Vocabulary Development Project: 31: Firwood Drive, Camberley, Surrey GU15 3QD (information about Makaton sign vocabulary and training).

● National Association for Special Educational Needs: NASEN House, 4/5 Amber Business Village, Amber Close, Amington, Tamworth, Staffordshire B77 4RP. Tel: 01827 311500. Website: www.nasen.org.uk.

● British Stammering Association: 15 Old Ford Road, Bethnal Green, London E2 9PJ.

USEFUL RESOURCES

● Acorn Educational Ltd: 32 Queen Eleanor Road, Geddington, Kettering, Northants NN14 1AY (equipment and resources including special needs).

● Ann Arbor Publishers: PO Box 1, Belford, Northumberland NE70 7JX (for books, assessment and learning resources that support learning disabilities).

● Anything Left-handed Ltd: 57 Brewer Street, London W1R 3FB. Tel: 020 74373910.

● The Learning Gym – Fun-to-Do Activities for Success at School by Erich Ballinger (Brain Gym), also available from Optimal Learning (page 95).

● Colour2C: though local, this website has useful information on visual dyslexia, Irlen syndrome and coloured filters. Website: www.colour2C.co.uk.

● Easylearn: Trent House, Fiskerton, Southwell, Nottinghamshire NG25 0UH. Website: www.easylearn.co.uk. (provides teaching materials that make learning easy).

● Fisher-Marriott Software: 58 Victoria Road, Woodbridge IP2 1EL. Tel: 01394 387050. Website: www.fishermarriott.com (for example, 'Starspell' software).

● Don Johnston Special Needs: 18/19, Clarendon Court, Calver Road, Winwick Quay, Warrington WA2 8QP. Tel: 01925 256500. Website: www.donjohnston.co.uk (produces the 'Solutions for Pupils with Special Needs' resource catalogue, full of intervention resources).

● Jolly Learning Ltd: Tailours House, High Road, Chigwell, Essex IG7 6DL. Tel: 0208 501 0405. Website: www.jollylearning.co.uk. (includes information on jolly phonics).

● LDA Primary and Special Needs catalogue: Duke Street, Wisbech, Cambridgeshire PE13 2AE. Tel: 01945 463441.

● Letterland Ltd: Collins Educational, HarperColins Publishers, Westerhill Road, Bishopbriggs, Glasgow G64 1BR.

● nfer Nelson produces a 'Specialist Assessment Catalogue'. Tel: 0845 6021937. Website: www.nfer-nelson.co.uk.

● The Psychological Corporation produces a catalogue of 'Educational Assessment & Intervention' resources. Tel: 01865 88188. Website: www.harcourt-uk.com.

● SBS (Step by Step): customer careline 0845 3001089 (toys and equipment for all special needs).

● Winslow 'Education & Special Needs' catalogue – see especially their resources on language support. Tel: 0845 9211777. Website: www.winslow-cat.com

● The Writers Press, USA publish a number of books for young children about a range of SEN. (Website:www.writerspress.com)